# DEDICATION

This publication is dedicated to Mervyn Tilley, chair of FOI for over forty years. His reach for the Lord was unfathomable, as he impacted the lives of so many people.  Henry Wadsworth Longfellow once wrote, '*When a great man dies, for years the light he leaves behind him, lies on the paths of men*'.  Mervyn's light will shine on the paths of men for years to come.

# CONTENTS

# INTRODUCTION

Each of us possess a world view that shapes our perception, values and actions. James Sire called it the 'discipleship of the mind'.

Culture and social environment often play a key role in shaping our interpretation and understanding of environmental issues, world politics, and religious belief. An example of this could be that our judgement of, 'what is, what should be and how things should be done', is often dependent upon the knowledge we already have, our mentors, people who we trust, our information source and our confidence in that source.

If we acknowledge this, we must be prepared to accept that people from different environments, may and probably will, perceive the world differently.

Problems arise when we limit our information base to existent biases, rather than considering those alternative sources and assessing their relevance and validity before making a decision.

*THUCYDIDES – 2500 BC – stated:*
*"Most people, in fact, will not take the trouble in finding out the truth, but are much more inclined to accept the first story they hear."*
*Thucydides, History of the Peloponnesian War.*

A dilemma that pervades our modern world, is actually, the opposite – 'information overload'. This may seem a paradox to what has just stated, but it is a real issue that we have to contend with. With the world wide web, Instagram, X, etc; the amount of information available to us now is staggering. Additionally, we live in a time where people are content to rely on sound bites, as opposed to taking time for in-depth consideration. Sadly though, much of the information disseminated contains cynical world views, biases against other people groups, historical disinformation or lack of nuance and empirical evidence.

Additionally, we live in an age where the differing truth claims made can seem reliable at the point of listening or reading. Often we can end up puzzled, perplexed, with not knowing what to believe or what the truth might be.

*"If you don't read the newspaper, you're uninformed. If you read the newspaper, you're mis-informed."*
*Mark Twain.*

This can be the case when attempting to undertake an historical analysis of Israel and Palestine. It is sometimes necessary to develop a sifting mechanism to eliminate potentially inaccurate, biased or unreliable information. Furthermore, we have to be mindful not to allow our existing social, cultural and religious influences to overly colour what we filter out. We must never permit truth to be subjugated by emotion. In spite of all of this, we believe it is possible to examine the information available and draft an accurate/balanced chronological summary of what we are witnessing right now.

## WHERE DO WE BEGIN?

It would be a mistake to consider this subject as just a modern issue, as some are apt to do. There is a long history, at least for the Jewish people. Added to this is the spiritual aspect to consider too. We will therefore break our discussion down into four distinct areas:

1. Ancient history - Pre-140 AD

2. The Diaspora - 140 AD - 1900 AD

3. Modern history - 1900 AD to present

4. Spiritual perspective

So, when discussing the current hostilities past history cannot be ignored or deemed irrelevant. Considering the past can inform us about present attitudes, ideologies and the differing opinions. Jews will reference their long association with the land when determining whether the modern state of Israel is an unwarranted occupier or a legitimate claimant. For evidence of this, they would refer to the Biblical narratives and archeological evidence. That is where we will begin.

“ To be or not to be
is not a question of compromise.
Either you be or you don't be. ”

*Golda Meir*

# Part One: Ancient History

## IT STARTED WITH AN INDIVIDUAL

In Genesis 11:31-32, we read the beginnings of the life story of Abram who originally lived in UR of the Chaldees. We are informed that his father Terah uplifted his family with the intention to move to the land of Canaan, but only got as far as Haran (Southern Turkey).

*Terah took Abram his son and Lot the son of Haran, his grandson, and Sarai his daughter-in-law, his son Abram's wife, and they went forth together from Ur of the Chaldeans to go into the land of Canaan, but when they came to Haran, they settled there. The days of Terah were 205 years, and Terah died in Haran. Genesis. 11:31-32*

Following Terah's death, Abram was instructed (In a vision from God) to leave Haran and take his immediate family to a location that God would give him and all his descendants in perpetuity. The land was in fact Canaan, the place that his father had intended to reside.

*The Lord had said to Abram, "Go from your country, your people and your father's household to the land I will show you. "I will make you into a great nation, and I will bless you; I will make your name great, and you will be a blessing. I will bless those who bless you, and whoever curses you I will curse; and all peoples on earth will be blessed through you." Genesis. 12:1-3*

Later God met with Abram to confirm His previous promise by making a divine covenant with him, promising both a blood heir and the land of Canaan.

*On that day the Lord made a covenant with Abram and said, "To your descendants I give this land, from the Wadi of Egypt to the great river, the Euphrates— the land of the Kenites, Kenizzites, Kadmonites, Hittites, Perizzites, Rephaites, Amorites, Canaanites, Girgashites and Jebusites." Genesis 15:18*

Eventually, Abraham did have two sons. Ishmael, born to Hagar, Sarah's handmaid, and Isaac, born to Sarah later in life. The Covenant passed down to Isaac, while Ishmael received a separate promise/covenant from God.

Abraham's acceptance of the promise of God, is afforded to him as an act of faith. It must be recognised though, that Abraham's journey of faith was not always a smooth one. Like most of us he had moments when he got things seriously wrong. Having a child with Sarah's handmaid, could be considered as one of them.

## ISHMAEL'S BLESSING

*The angel of the Lord told her, "Go back to your mistress and submit to her." The angel added, "I will increase your descendants so much that they will be too numerous to count." The angel of the Lord also said to her: "You are now pregnant and you will give birth to a son. You shall name him Ishmael, for the Lord has heard of your misery. He will be a wild donkey of a man; his hand will be against everyone and everyone's hand against him, and he will live in hostility toward all his brothers." Genesis 16:9-11 (also See 17:20).*

Historically, the original Muslims viewed themselves as the descendants of Ishmael, with Muhammed being a direct ancestor. For this reason, Muslims trace their blessing back to Abraham and his covenant through Ishmael, as opposed to Isaac. While not all Arabs are Muslim and not all Muslims are Arabs, this would be the case for majority of Palestinian Arabs.

## ISAAC'S BLESSING

*Then God said, "Yes, but your wife Sarah will bear you a son, and you will call him Isaac. I will establish my covenant with him as an everlasting covenant for his descendants after him. Genesis 17:19.*

Isaac also went on to have two sons - Esau and Jacob. (twins). The narratives inform us that there was enmity between them even in the womb.

*The Lord said to her, "Two nations are in your womb, and two peoples from within you will be separated; one people will be stronger than the other, and the older will serve the younger."*
*When the time came for her to give birth, there were twin boys in her womb. The first to come out was red, and his whole body was like a hairy garment; so they named him Esau. After this, his brother came out, with*

*his hand grasping Esau's heel; so he was named Jacob.*
*Genesis 25:23-26.*

By tradition the blessing should have passed down to Esau who was the eldest, but God chose the Covenant agreement to Pass onto Jacob (whose name was later changed to Israel).

## IT THEN BECAME A FAMILY

A large family grew up around Jacob, as he had 12 sons. The latter part of Genesis and the book of Exodus informs us of their story.

Many would know the story of Joseph, Jacob's beloved son, who was cruelly betrayed by his brothers and sold to Egyptian slave traders. Due to famine, the family were forced to travel to Egypt, where the son who Jacob thought had died, was now second in command. In Egypt Israel's family grew exponentially, and after a period of 400 years, Exodus 12:40, the Egyptians had forgotten the positive impact of Joseph, and now feared their presence and influence on the Egyptian society.

The family of Israel became slaves to the Egyptians and a concerted period of persecution ensued, Exodus 1:8.

Again, many readers would be aware of the story of the Exodus. Moses, a Jewish boy raised as a Pharaoh, is then given by God the task of setting the people of Israel free and leading them back into the land originally promised to Abraham and his descendants.

*"Go, assemble the elders of Israel and say to them, 'The Lord, the God of your fathers— the God of Abraham, Isaac and Jacob— appeared to me and said: I have watched over you and have seen what has been done to you in Egypt. And I have promised to bring you up out of your misery in Egypt into the land of the Canaanites, Hittites, Amorites, Perizzites, Hivites and Jebusites—a land flowing with milk and honey.'*
*Exodus 3:16-17.*

From a human perspective, it is an epic story of divine intervention and human struggle to release the bonds of oppression and become a nation with a land of their own and self-determination.

*And who is like your people Israel—the one nation*

*on earth that God went out to redeem as a people for himself, and to make a name for himself, and to perform great and awesome wonders by driving out nations and their gods from before your people, whom you redeemed from Egypt? You have established your people Israel as your very own forever, and you, Lord, have become their God. 2 Samuel 7:23-24.*

## THE FAMILY BECAME A NATION

The overall theme of the books of Exodus, Deuteronomy, Leviticus and Numbers, is God establishing a people group through which he will fulfil His divine work of salvation for mankind. For God, they are a chosen people and a holy nation, for a divine purpose.

*"You yourselves have seen what I did to the Egyptians, and how I bore you on eagles' wings and brought you to myself. Now therefore, if you will indeed obey my voice and keep my covenant, you shall be my treasured possession among all peoples, for all the earth is mine; 6and you shall be to me a kingdom of priests and a holy nation.' These are the words that you shall speak to the people of Israel.". Exodus 19:4-6.*

## ISRAEL BECAME A NATION WITH A LAND

During the previous 400 years, Canaan had been repopulated with a diverse number of people groups. Israel had to do battle with these groups to establish pre-eminence. It took about 350 years, 13 generations. It was not until the reign of David that the Jewish people achieved this. Although he initially still faced battles with some people groups, most prominently the Philistines. David won out, and greatly increased the area that the Israelites controlled. It was only really then, that the whole region became known as the Land of Israel, with Jerusalem its capital.

*David then took up residence in the fortress and called it the City of David. He built up the area around it, from the terraces inward. And he became more and more powerful, because the Lord God Almighty was with him. 2 Samuel 5:6-10.*

This took place around 1000 BC, which would mean that Israel had control of the land as early as 3,000 years ago.

David's son Solomon, continued the expansion, security and dominance of the nation of Israel. Solomon improved David's citadel and built a permanent Temple for national worship in the heart of the Capital.

*Then Solomon began to build the temple of the Lord in Jerusalem on Mount Moriah, where the Lord had appeared to his father David. It was on the threshing floor of Araunah the Jebusite, he place provided by David.  Chronicles 3:1.*

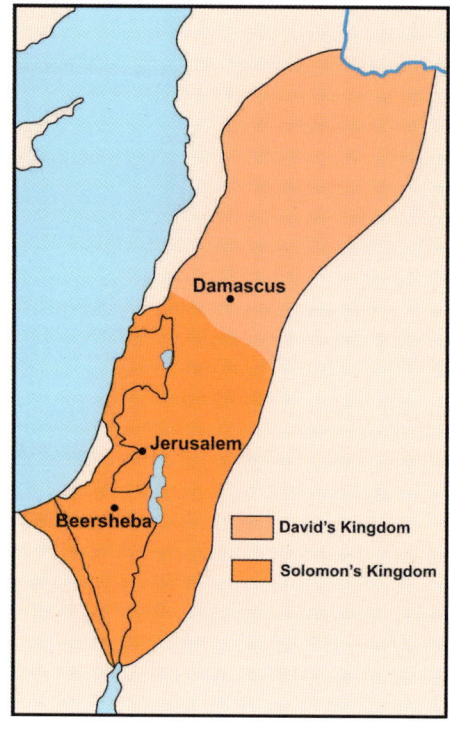

Following the death of Solomon, his son Rehoboam took his place, but because of high taxation and the use of Israelite people as slaves to the king, his brother revolted with the support of 10 tribes. This left Rehoboam with only Judah and the tribe of Benjamin supporting him.

The 10 northern tribes set their capital in Shechem, and retained the name Israel.

Rehoboam remained in Jerusalem and his region was renamed Judah. The land had become a two-state nation.  (930.BC).

*Then Ahijah laid hold of the new garment that was on him, and tore it into twelve pieces. And he said to Jeroboam, "Take for yourself ten pieces, for thus says the Lord, the God of Israel, 'Behold, I am about to tear the kingdom from the hand of Solomon and will give you ten tribes (but he shall have one tribe, for the sake of my servant David and for the sake of Jerusalem, the city that I have chosen out of all the tribes of Israel).*
*1 Kings 11: 30-32*

## ISRAEL & JUDAH EXILED

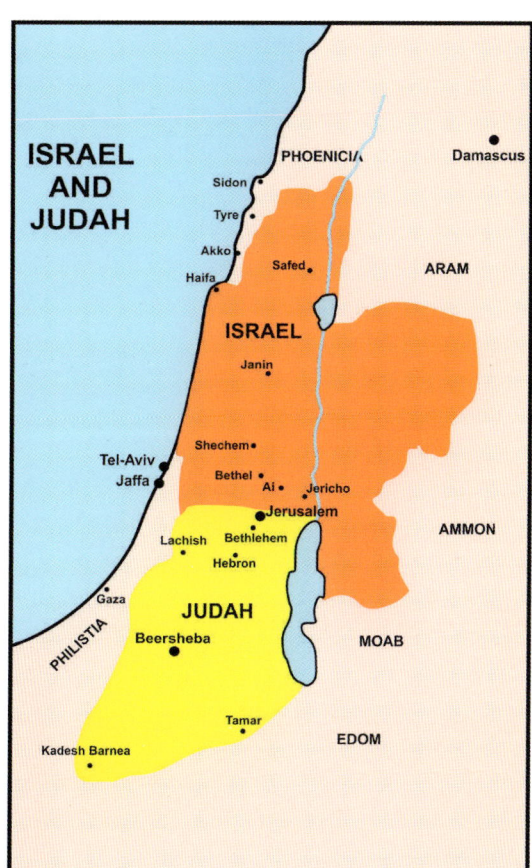

For the next 200 years they were ruled separately. Israel had 19 kings across 9 dynasties, but eventually fell to the Assyrians in about 722BC.

Judah had 20 kings over a period of about 450 years, until they were overthrown by Babylon. A common practice was to exile the nobility back to Babylon for retraining, and leave the poor behind. Additionally, they then migrated other conquered people groups and coalesced them with the remaining population. According to tradition, the Samaritans evolved from these amalgamated people.

After 70 years of exile, the Jews were permitted to return to their capital and rebuild their nation, but still under subjugation. Life for the early settlers was difficult and they faced considerable opposition from the existing Samaritan dwellers.

Despite the initial hostility, the post exilic Jews did overcome and re-establish themselves into the land, and eventually achieving semi-independence, naming the new state

Judah. In place of a king, the people were now governed by a priestly dynasty who instilled Torah observance.

## ISRAEL SUBJUGATED BUT REMAIN IN THE LAND

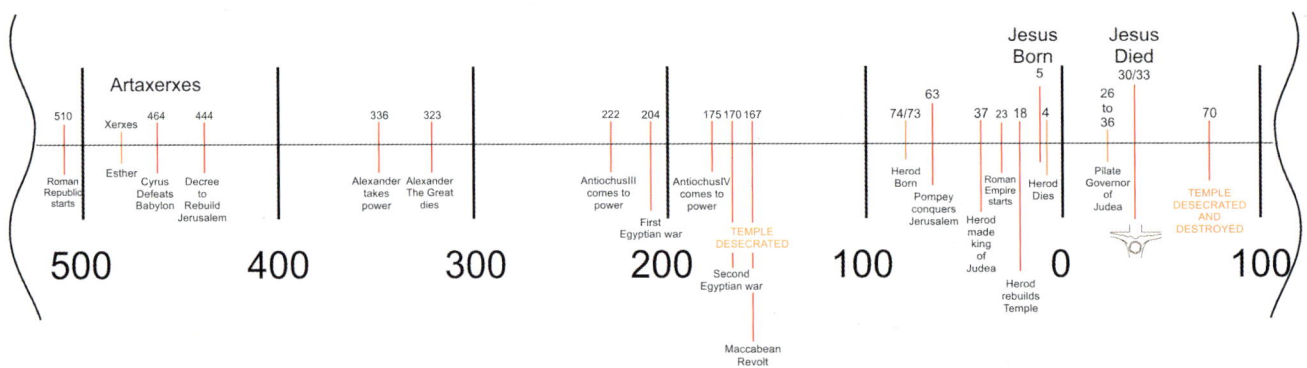

Over the next 400 years, Judah came under the blanket control of a succession of dominant nations such as the Persians, Macedonians, Hasmoneans and then eventually the Romans. They did enjoy independence for a short time following their defeat of Antiochus IV (Epiphanes), around 173 B.C.

Shortly after the Romans came to power, Herod the great was permitted to govern Israel in 40 BC, and in 6 AD it became the Roman province of Ludaea. During his reign, Herod rebuilt the temple in Jerusalem with great magnificence.  In addition though he also built the Fortress Antonia, which over shadowed the temple, along with public baths, a theater, amphitheater and hippodrome.  The introduction  of these foreign activities were not liked by many, however, the priestly rulers sought to maintain a level of cordiality with Rome.

In return the Romans afforded the Jewish priesthood a certain level of religious freedom, but life under the Romans for ordinary people was pretty harsh. Taxation was heavy and there was always the presence of military control. As a result tensions constantly existed within the province. In the course of time this led to two separate Jewish rebellions. The first was between 66-70 AD.

In AD 64. A turning point that sparked Jewish resistance, was the brutality of Gessius Florus, the newly appointed procurator for Judea. In 66 AD All out rebellion ensued with the zealots managing to take control of the city. when Florus returned to Rome, the Jews proceeded to gain control of Galilee in the north and some of the southern territories. Caesar Nero appointed Vespasian to take care of the situation. Placing his son Titus in command, the Roman legions swept through the land quickly regaining control until they came to Jerusalem. He immediately placed a siege around the city. As a result of a final and brutal conflict, both Herod's Temple and Jerusalem were destroyed, and many of its residents were taken as slaves.

This was not the end though. A group of fugitives made their way to the Herodian mountain fortress of Masada, in the Dead sea region. They held out against the 49th legion for three more years. It was finally brought to a tragic end with the mass suicide of all but one of its inhabitants.

**The Hasmonaean Kingdom
(Maccabees 167 BC)**

Without the Temple, the Jewish life and worship was dramatically effected. Resilient as ever, the Jewish people turned to the local synagogue system to become the heart of the community and created rabbinical Judaism. It is a system that proved to be transportable for wherever they were.

Jerusalem laid mainly untouched until 130AD. In that year, Hadrian passed by Jerusalem and decided to raze it to the ground and build a new Roman-style city centered on Roman worship. He also decreed a ban on Jewish circumcision. This proved too much for the Jews still living in the land.

In 132AD a second rebellion was led by Simon Bar Kokhba. Rabbi Akkiva declared him as the Messiah King who would usher in the

promised new messianic age. He was an able military leader who initially defeated two Roman legions. He took over the Herodian Fortress and declared independence for the New state of Judah.

Hadrian's response was to embark on a full-scale Judean offensive in 134 AD, putting an end, once and for all, to any foreseeable Jewish insurrection within the region.

## JEWS ARE EXPELLED AND ISRAEL IS RENAMED

The Bar Kokhba revolt was the last straw for the Romans who proceeded to banish all Jewish people from the land. This was not for the first time, but it would prove to be the longest.

A Diaspora of Jewish people quickly spread throughout Iraq, Yemen, Europe, and North Africa including, Ethiopia, Egypt, Morocco, Algeria.

Emperor Hadrian pressed on with his plans to rename the region of Israel, calling it Syria Palaestina, and the city of Jerusalem to Aelia Capitolina.

This was the first time that the region was ever associated with the name Palestine, and it was intended as an insult to Jewish people by renaming it after their historical enemies, the Philistines.

The city maintained the named Aelia Capitolina until the Council of Chalcedon in

451 AD, when it was put back to Jerusalem. However, they kept regional name as Palestine.

"As I watch what is happening in the Middle East and the carnage that comes over our television screens every evening, I cannot help but ask myself, what is wrong with humankind that we cannot stop the killing?

*Marcy Kaptur*

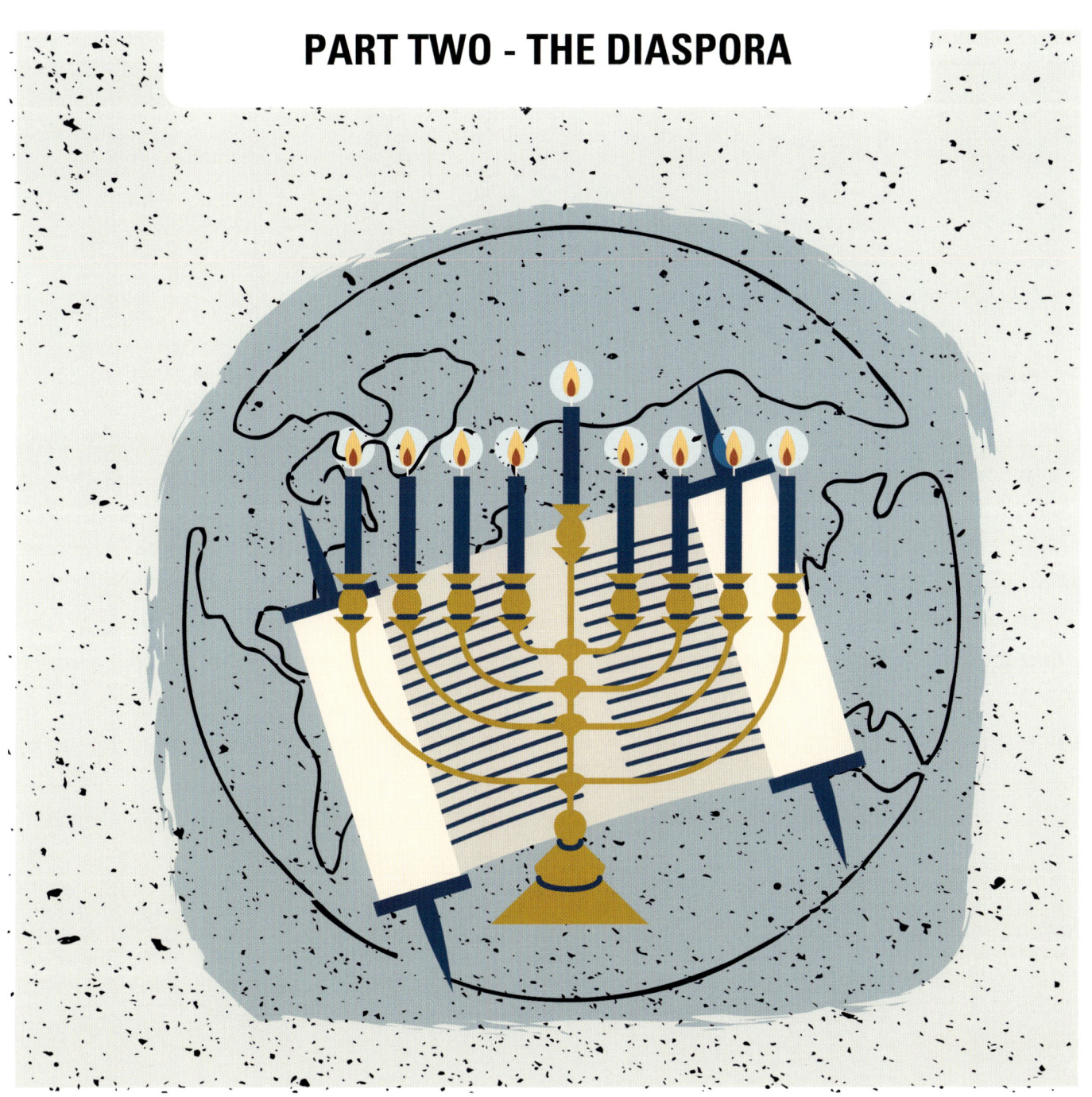

# PART TWO - THE DIASPORA

## A PERSECUTED PEOPLE

Some Jewish people did return to the land to live as soon as they could, quietly settling in Galilee and the more northern areas. Others returned only once a year on the permitted day of Tisha Be-Av (day of mourning for the Temple). Many more though, remained in the diaspora never to return.

While separated from the land, Jewish people took great care to maintain their identity, faith and cultural integrity. In addition to the Torah, the Rabbinical oral laws were codified for the first time in the Mishnah, which described how Jewish people were to live.

Their lifestyle, code of dress, and religious laws often became an isolating factor for them from the immediate communities in which they lived, and as a result they often suffered greatly over the next 1800 years.

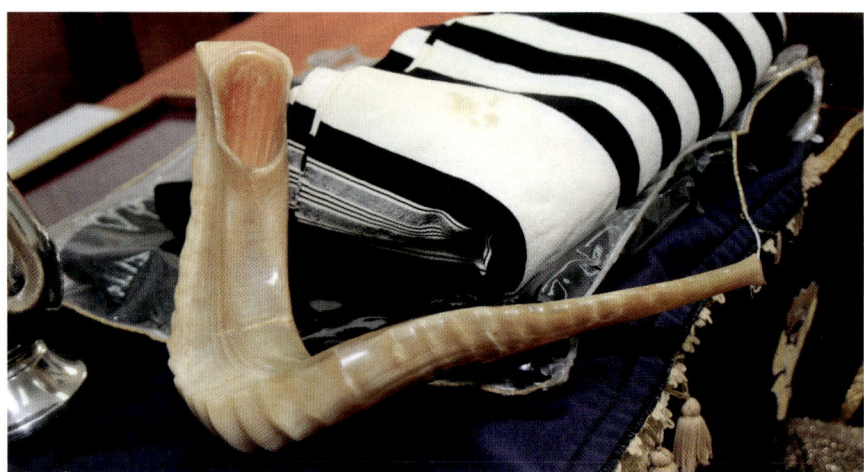

Religious persecution led to separation, vilification, dehumanization, torture, mass murders, forced conversions, and expulsions from one nation to another.

In the latter centuries with the emergence of the age of enlightenment, one would have thought that persecution of the Jews would have waned, but this was not to be the case. Modern secularist states, most notably in Eastern Europe, turned on them too. One example would be the Russian pogroms in the 19th century. There was no respite.

## PALESTINE

In the intervening years, Palestine fell into the hands of various controlling powers.

The Romans maintained Jerusalem's importance by incorporating it as a part of their Mediterranean trade route. With the conversion of Constantine to Christianity in the 4th century, Israel and Jerusalem once again became a spiritual focal point, with many sacred buildings being erected. The Romans remained in control until the 6th century.

It was in the late 6th century, that there emerged the new religion of Islam. Its prophet Mohammed quickly managed to unite the Arab peoples, and they conquered Palestine in around 640 A.D.

Within a short space of time, the Muslims constructed two principal Islamic religious buildings on the Temple Mount in Jerusalem; the Al Asqa Mosque and the Dome of the Rock, making Jerusalem an important strategic Islamic place.

They remained in control of the land until the 11th century, when it fell back in to the hands of the Christians, following the European Christian campaign, more commonly known as the Crusades. The battles for control of Palestine and Jerusalem lasted for about two centuries, until the Muslims finally managed to win it back, and eventually it came under the Egyptian Mamluks in around 1250 AD.

The Mamluk's hold on Palestine continued until the 16th century, when the Ottoman Turks invaded and replaced them. Their reign lasted until 20th century.

## A DREAM TO RETURN TO THE LAND

It was not until the 19th century that Jewish people began to seriously consider the possibility of returning to their homeland to restore a Jewish state, and remove the shackles of oppression. In the late 19th century Theodor Herzl created the Zionist movement, with this aim in mind.

The first international congress was held in Basal, Switzerland, on August 29–31, 1897. All told there were Two hundred and eight delegates who attended from seventeen different countries.

The congress established the following goals: Zionism seeks to establish a home in Palestine for the Jewish people, secured under public law. To achieve this goal, the Congress envisages the following means:

1. The expedient promotion of the settlement of Jewish agriculturists, artisans, and businessmen in Palestine.

2. The organization and bringing together of all Jews through local and general events, according to the laws of the various countries.

3. The strengthening of Jewish feeling and national consciousness.

4. Preparatory steps for obtaining the governmental approval which is necessary to the achievement of the Zionist purpose.

Encouraged by this, the first wave of Jewish settlers began to migrate to Palestine. They purchased ground and worked the land. It did not go well for many of them, with a considerable number suffering from swamp disease, malaria and hunger.

Additionally, due to the absence of many Jewish people over the previous 1800 years, Palestine had become largely populated by Muslim Arabs, Christian Arabs and other Christian people groups. Many resented the influx of the Jewish settlers.

So, as in Moses' day, when they returned to the Land, other people lived there. Equally similar though, these existing communities were often small and dotted all over the place, with most of it being undeveloped.

"I ask to remember the sufferings of the Jewish people all over the world. I ask to remember that Palestine, of all the places in the world, was certainly the place where they had some right to expect not to suffer or to have restrictions imposed upon them."

*Herbert Stanley Morrison,*
*Baron Morrison of Lambeth.*

Foreign Office,
November 2nd, 1917.

Dear Lord Rothschild,

I have much pleasure in conveying to you, on behalf of His Majesty's Government, the following declaration of sympathy with Jewish Zionist aspirations which has been submitted to, and approved by, the Cabinet

His Majesty's Government view with favour the establishment in Palestine of a national home for the Jewish people, and will use their best endeavours to facilitate the achievement of this object, it being clearly understood that nothing shall be done which may prejudice the civil and religious rights of existing non-Jewish communities in Palestine, or the rights and political status enjoyed by Jews in any other country'

I should be grateful if you would bring this declaration to the knowledge of the Zionist Federation.

Yours,

Arthur James Balfour

# PART THREE - MODERN HISTORY

## THE BRITISH MANDATE

During the first world war, the British went on the offensive in Egypt and the Palestinian region driving out the Ottomans, and by 1918 they were in control. It was at this time that the British government began to put their weight behind the idea of a renewed state in Palestine, and produced a key document in 1917, that would have great significance. It was called 'The Balfour Declaration, and it set out their intention to re-establish a Jewish state back in their former homeland, while also seeking to protect the rights of those already living there.

These intentions were confirmed after the war by the League of Nations, which was the forerunner to the United Nations, in 1920 with the SAN REMO Agreement. Plans were drawn up giving the new state of Israel much more territory than it has now.

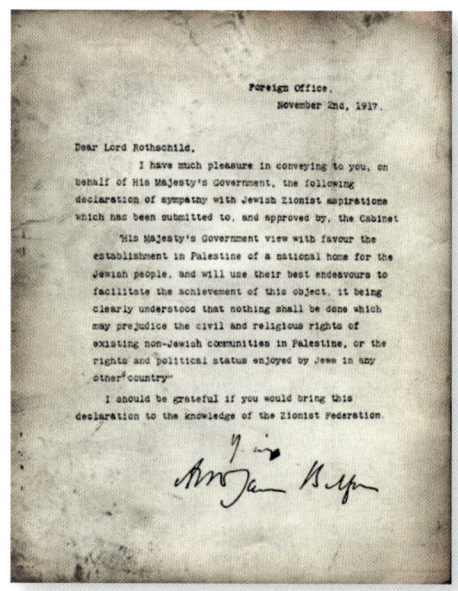

To allay the Arab communities fears, Britain later declared their plans to create an independent Hashemite Kingdom of Jordan. However the hostilities simply got worse. Winston Churchill, who was at the time the British Colonial Secretary declared...."Both Arabs and Jews are armed and ... ready to spring at each other's throats".

The 1929 'The Wailing Wall' riots, was in some way a turning point for the Jews, who increased their demand for an independent state. In most instances, the riots involved Arabs attacking Jews and destroying their property. During the week of riots, from 23 to 29 August, 133 Jews were killed by Arabs, and 339 Jews were injured, most of whom were unarmed.

During the 1930's the influx of Jewish people increased dramatically due to the growing persecution in Germany and other European countries. The British response was to set up a detention camp in Atlit on the west coast, to detain illegal Jewish immigrants. This sparked reprisals from Jews already living in the land.

The Arabs responded to the Jewish influx by intensifying their attacks on the Jewish settlers, which was reciprocated with equal force. The British authorities frustratingly found themselves being caught in the middle.

The 1930 white paper-Hope Simpson Report noted that thousands of Arabs were also immigrating into Palestine for work. It stated that illegal Arab immigration was an 'injustice' that was displacing prospective Jewish settlers.
*(From Time Immemorial-Joan Peters- 296-297).*

In 1936 the Mufti of Jerusalem called for a general strike against the British Administration which led to a 3-year violent revolt. As a response to the Arab uprising, Britain produced a second white paper on their suggested future for Palestine. It was radically different from the original Balfour Declaration and the San Remo Agreement.

1. A bi-national independent state of Palestine for both Jews and Arabs, with the majority having control. To be established within 10 Years.

2. The Limit of Jewish quotas to 75,000 over a five-year period.

3. The protection of the rights of Jewish people.

Following the first World War, Germany's economy declined drastically under the Weimar Republic. This paved the way for Hitler's rise to power, who blamed the Jews for the woes of their country. Jewish people once again, began facing a fresh wave of marginalisation and persecution.

## HELL ON EARTH FOR JEWISH PEOPLE

The second World War, brought to a head the tumultuous and unmerited hatred for Jewish people, witnessing the horrific genocide and massacre of over 6 million Jewish people.

The end of the war revealed the true horror of the atrocities perpetrated by Germany, supported by their allies, which included the Mufti of Jerusalem, Amin al-Husseini. Shock and revulsion reverberated throughout the world, with verbal recognition of a need to give Jewish people a place of safety and a homeland of their own. All eyes were on the Land of Palestine for this to be created.

Despite this, persecution of Jewish holocaust victims continued. The British Government tried to prevent Jewish survivors from entering Palestine.

In 1947 the Exodus, an old Packet Steamship made its way from France to Palestine with about 4,500 holocaust survivors on board. All of them were without certificates of entrance. The British Navy boarded the ship while it was still in international waters and led it to the port of Haifa.

On July 18th, there was a struggle between the passengers and British soldiers. Three Jewish people were killed, and dozens were injured. After a few weeks the British government forcibly had them sent back to France, and then immediately on to a concentration camp in Hamburg, Germany. The fall out and public shame for the British brought the ongoing plight of the Jewish people to the surface, and the immediate international recognition of the need for Jewish people to have a homeland of their own. But where?

## POST WAR – A NATION IS BORN

In 1946 the League of Nations was Liquidated and was superseded by The United Nations. The problem of Palestine was immediately handed over to them. It was decided that Britain would relinquish its mandate over the region by 1st August 1948 Two independent states would be created with clear boundaries, within two months of British departure. This was passed in 29th Nov 1947.

One was for the Jewish people, and to be called Israel, the other was for the Arab people and to be called Trans-Jordan.

It must be understood that in the eyes of the British and the United Nations, the Arab dwellers were not considered uniquely as Palestinians at that time. In fact, from the time that Hadrian renamed the region to the mid-20th century, there is no evidence that this was ever the case.  Two Weeks Later Britain announced that the mandate would terminate on 15th May 1948.

Both communities were offered a free democratic state, with the right to self-determination. The Arab League objected to this, but the Jewish community accepted it. On midnight 14th May 1948, the State of Israel declared Its independence.

The Arab league backed by the amalgamated armies of Egypt, Jordan, Lebanon, Syria and

Iraq, declared war. They were confident that it would be a quickly fought battle, with the eradication of all Jews in the land.
The Secretary-General of the Arab League, Azzam Pasha, was recorded by Akhbar el-Yom newspaper, *"This war,"* he said, *"will be a war of extermination and a momentous massacre which will be spoken of like the Mongol massacres and the Crusades."*

To everyone's surprise, Israel came out victorious and emerged as a new nation, which was recognised by many in the international community and the U.N.

The Arab community living there, as well as many Arab nations who had attacked them, refused to do so.

The Land became divided into the following areas:

1. Trans-Jordan (including part of the West Bank of the Jordan river and Jerusalem).

2. The Central State of Israel

3. Egypt establishing an Arab protectorate in the Gaza Strip.

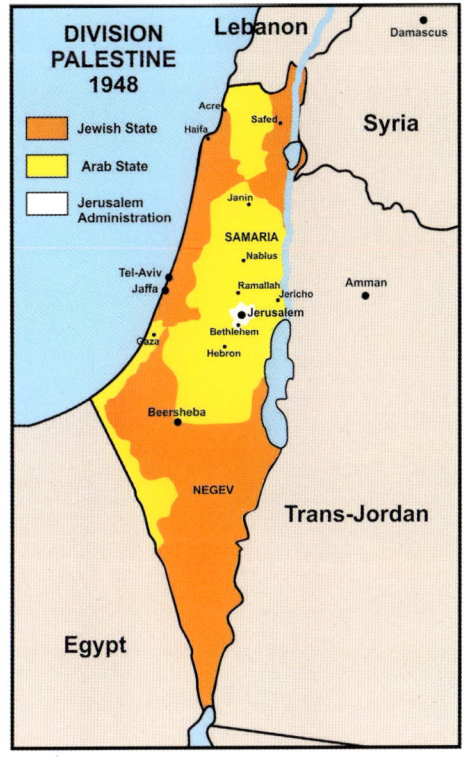

All with clearly defined borders.

The war saw the displacement of quite a number of Arabs living in the Land. Some official documents have estimated it possibly as much as 650,000. The Arabs called this 'the Nakba', and accused Israel for their plight. Later inspection though of additional documents, appear to indicate that the figure is much lower. Additionally, it must be noted, that there is evidence to show that while there were expulsions by Israelis, the majority of Arab refugees appear to have left of their own volition following the advice of surrounding Arab nations, so that they could go in and destroy Israel. The promise was that they could return after the event. Of course, this never happened, because Israel prevailed, and so the Arabs were left homeless and in limbo.

In his memoirs, Haled al-Azm, Prime Minister of Syria, wrote; *"Since 1948, we have been demanding the return of the refugees to their homes. But we ourselves are the ones who encouraged them to leave. Only a few months separated our call to them to leave and our appeal to the United Nations to resolve their return".*

In his book 'Ma'na al Nakba, The meaning of Disaster', Constantine Zureiq, defines the Nakba as, *' The seven Arab states declaring war on Zionism, stopping impotent before it, and then turning on their heels'.* It was only in the late 1980's that the Arabs chose to recoin the term to mean an Israeli-inflicted injustice.

Every Arab that chose to stay in the newly created nation of Israel, was offered Israeli citizenship with full and equal rights. That remains the case today. Currently there are 2.1million Israeli Arabs, and they account for 21% of the population.

There is no doubt that both sides committed atrocities during the war of independence, and their descendants still carry the scars and memories that affect their thinking today.

## IMPORTANT QUESTION TO CONSIDER

One has to ask the question, if Jordan and Egypt had complete control of the West Bank, Jerusalem and the Gaza Strip between 1948 – 1967, why did they not give the land to the displaced Arabs who had lived in Palestine and help them create a new independent Arab nation called Palestine?
Remember, the New nation of Israel had already accepted the U.N's two-state solution. Why did the U.N not work for that outcome either?

## PALESTINIAN DILEMMA FOR THE UNITED NATIONS

In 1950, the United Nations established the UNRWA, a unique department for Arab refugees. One of its initial reports published in 1961, stated that it was impossible to exclude nomadic Bedouin's, or local residents from genuine Palestinian refugees. In many cases 'individuals who could not qualify as being bona fide refugees are in fact on the relief roles'. As early as the 1950's they knew the Palestinian number of refugees was over exaggerated by as much as 100,000 people. Between 1948-67, Israel faced increasing threats from neighbouring Arab states. In 1964 the Palestinian Liberation Organisation was created. More on this later.

*What was initially considered as the Jewish plight by the world, quickly turned into an Arab Palestinian Plight. Jewish people, once again became the punch bag for the world.*

What we see now, is a geographical region that has become doubly promised by world powers. First for the Jewish people so that they could have a place of freedom and safety; and then secondly, as a consequence, for Arab Palestinians too. Hence their desire to create a two state Solution, which has not worked. Ultimately, when you have people groups living in the land who reject this solution in favour for a single state, violence will reign.

Despite all of this; no one can deny the miracle of Israel becoming a nation in such a short space of time, in fact, literally overnight. For this reason, many believe, that only the God of Israel could have made this happen, and is a fulfilment of Biblical prophecy.

The majority of land that was designated to Israel was either Swamp, wilderness or desert. However, through the ingenuity, skill and determination, the people of Israel began to develop and transform the Land. Again, another prophetic fulfilment.-

*He turns a desert into pools of water, a parched land into springs of water. And there he lets the hungry dwell, and they establish a city to live in; they sow fields and plant vineyards and get a fruitful yield. By his blessing they multiply greatly, and he does not let their livestock diminish.*
*Psalm 107:35–38.*

It is important to note, that it was not the Arabs alone who faced displacement in 1948. Hundreds of thousands of Jewish people were expelled from many of the Arab nations, and became refugees without a home. Naturally, most of those expelled fled to Israel.
An article even appeared in the New York Times on 16 May 1948 titled 'Jews at grave risk in Muslim lands: Nine hundred thousand

Africans and Asians face wrath from their foes'.

| 1948 JEWISH REFUGEES FROM ARAB COUNTRIES | |
| --- | --- |
| Morocco - | 265,000 |
| algeria - | 140,000 |
| Iraq - | 135,000 |
| Tunisia - | 105,000 |
| Egypt - | 75,000 |
| Yemen - | 63,000 |
| Lybia - | 38,000 |
| Syria - | 30,000 |
| Lebanon - | 5,000 |

## THE RISE OF THE PALESTINIAN LIBERATION ORGANISATION

Between 1948-1967, the emerging State of Israel faced increasing threats from neighbouring Arab States.

In 1964, as already stated, the Palestinian Liberation Organisation (PLO), was founded during the Arab League Summit, Cairo. Its aim was to right the wrongs suffered by displaced Palestinian Arabs, by establishing an Arab State over the entire region of the former British Mandate, with the right for all refugees to return. At its heart, was actually, the elimination of the State of Israel in order to create the State of Palestine in its place. They proffered that Jews could not be considered as a nation because it was a religion, therefore have no single nationality. They were simply citizens of States to which they belong. (Palestinian National charter, 1968). The more vocal this organisation became the more support it received from the Arab States.

# INTERNATIONAL TENSIONS:
# A LAND UNDER CONFLICT

In the background to this was the Suez Canal crisis.

In 1956, the Egyptian President Gamal Nassar sought to nationalise the Suez Canal and Tiran Strait. Conflict ensued when the UK, France and Israel immediately attacked Egypt and eventually the U.N, was given the responsibility to control the routes. Despite small skirmishes between Israel and Its neighbour States the next 10 years were on the whole fairly calm.

In 1967, Gamal Nassar expelled the UN from Egypt and closed the Straits of Tiran to Israel, as well as signing a defence treaty with Jordan. At the same time, the Soviet Union claimed that Israel was about to attack Syria.

On 5th June 1967, Israel launched a pre-emptive air strike against Syria and Egypt, decimating both of their air forces. They then proceeded to do the same to Iraq and Jordan. By the end of that day, they had secured military air control over the whole region.

Israel then proceeded to embark on a ground assault in the Sinai Peninsula and the Gaza Strip. In support of Egypt, Jordan entered the conflict by firing on Israel from East Jerusalem. Israel immediately responded with a comprehensive counter-attack.  A third front then opened up in the north with Syria attacking from the Golan Heights.

The combat continued for the next five days and by the end of it, Israel had secured control of East Jerusalem, the Temple Mount, the West Bank, Gaza and the Golan Heights. These are now what are called the occupied territories.

For the first time in 2000 years the Jewish people had access to the Temple Mount. It was an incredible moment that they had prayed for every day since its demise in 70AD. Surprisingly and with great criticism from religious Jews both then and now Moshe Dyan, Israeli Minister of Defence, within hours of its capture, chose to hand back the Temple Mount to the Muslims.

He pronounced:

*"We have returned to the holiest of our places, never to be parted from them again....We did not come to conquer the sacred sites of others or to restrict their religious rights, but rather to ensure the integrity of the city and to live in it with others in fraternity."*

Following the Six Day War, the Arab nations were again left in total shock. Israel emerged as a different and much stronger nation. The rest of the world were equally stunned and in complete awe. No one could have believed that such a small and emergent nation could have wrought such a victory. Instead, they had expected their demise.

## INTERNATIONAL PRESSURE:
## A DIVIDED LAND

On the heels of victory, Israel was faced with a different problem. The control of the additional Land that brought with it more than a million Palestinian Arabs. It is said that around 100,000 fled during the conflict increasing the number of those falling under the UN's refugee status, and a fresh call to free the Palestinian people from oppression by Israel.

How were they going to treat these new occupants, and what would their status be?

It would appear that the East Jerusalem Arabs were offered immediate citizenship, but not many of the Arabs who lived within the West Bank. However, this was declined by majority of Jerusalem Arabs, preferring instead to keep their Jordanian citizenship. Alternatively, they were given a permanent resident status. This way it continued the non-co-operation with Israel and provided them with a new status of living under the condition of a hostile and illegitimate occupier of their Land.

This started the PLO's demands for a free Palestine and increased their legitimacy, and influence, especially among the Palestinian Arabs

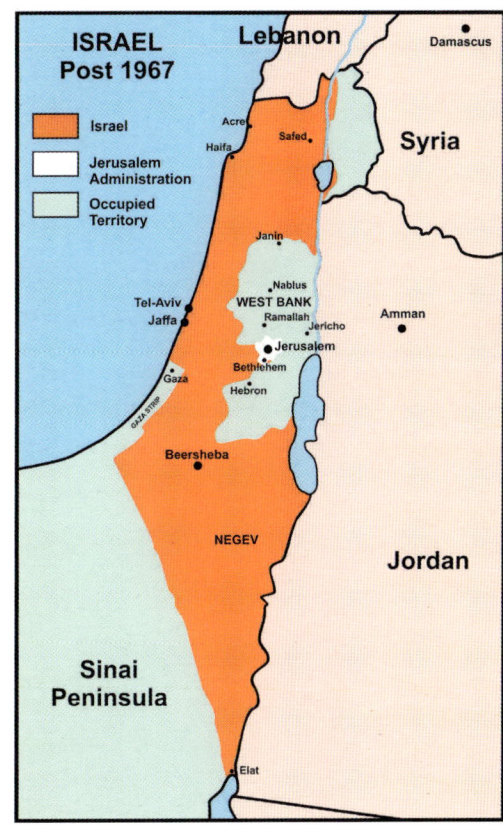

International pressure was being placed on Israel and the surrounding Arab nations to seek a solution to create a lasting peace.

## UNITED NATIONS RESOLUTION 242

In response to the Six Day War, the U.N. Security Council met to discuss the problem of the Middle-East. What resulted was Resolution 242, which demanded two following directives.

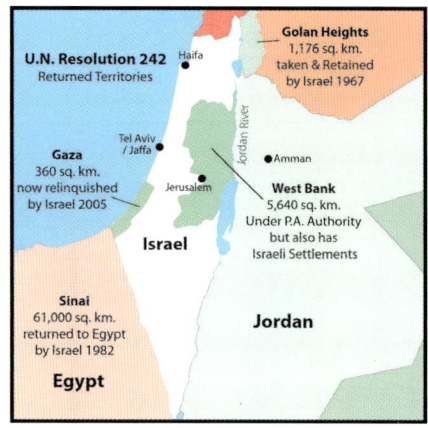

1. Israel should withdraw armed forces from the territories occupied in the Six Day War.

2. The ceasing of all acts of Violence and the acknowledgement of the rights and independence of every State in the region.

3. The right for all to live in peace.

4. The establishment and recognition of clear and secure borders, that are free from threat.

5. A just settlement for Palestinian refugees.

6. Free access to international waters.

Three of the nations, Israel, Egypt and Jordan accepted the resolution, with Syria rejecting it, as it believed that Israel had to withdraw back to pre-Six Day War lines, before any talks of peace were entered in to. The PLO, chose to side with Syria, in light of Jordan relinquishing its claims on the West Bank and deciding to hand all rights to the Palestinian People.

## CONTINUED CONFLICT

In 1973, there came another war. On 6th October, which happened to be the day of the Jewish Yom Kippur for that year, a coalition of Arab forces led by Egypt and Syria, made a surprise coordinated attack. The Egyptians from the Sinai Peninsula, and the Syrians on the Golan Heights. Their initial objectives were to take both of these regions back following their loss in the 1967 war.

The initial surprise enabled the advancing forces to make considerable gains. Following three days of intense battles, Israel though managed to halt the advancements on both fronts. Israel sought support from the US, but initially it was rejected, until Russia added its support to Syria.

From that point on Israel was able to successfully go on the counter-attack and push the opposing armies back. The U.N tried several times to arrange a cease fire without success, however increased international pressure ended the fighting on 26 October.

It is generally considered that Israel once again, gained the upper hand, and more territory, but it did not come without a price.

Official peace was not achieved with Egypt until 1979, with the historic Camp David Accords. At which point Israel returned the Sinai Peninsula, and diplomatic relations were opened.

Syria fared the worst from the war partly due to Egypt's early cease fire with Israel. It now enabled Israel to focus on the northern frontier, dealing Syria a heavy blow and gaining more territory. As a consequence of this, Syria's relationship with Egypt completely broke down.

Following Egypt's treaty with Israel in 1979, Syria pushed for Egypt to be expelled from the Arab League.

# INTERNAL CONFLICT

With Israel coming out on top again, the PLO realised that they could not rely on the military superiority of the neighbouring armies to come to their aid. They had to review their strategy. Focus was now on freeing the occupied territories by any means and establishing their own independent authority. This included acts of terrorism against both military and civilian Israeli targets.

Following the Yom Kippur War there were several accords to try and broker a peace between Israel and Egypt.

1 The Sinai, agreement in 1975
2 The camp David Accords in 1978

Eventually peace was achieved in 1979, following which, Israel handed back the Sinai Peninsula, and Egypt created a border between them and Gaza. It became known as the Philadelphi Route.

Despite this, the Middle-East was a potential powder keg waiting to explode. Israel continued to face aggression on its northern border with Lebanon and Syria, supported by the PLO, who also now had a military wing. Israel declared Jerusalem to be its capital, and Hebron was reopened for Jewish people to live, provoking more terrorist attacks.

Throughout the eighties tensions with the neighbours continued, including the Lebanon war, and more and more internal acts of terrorism.

In 1987, following the 1st intifada, a small Islamist group named Hamas (in Arabic means – Zeal or bravery, but in Hebrew it means violence and is used about 30 times in O.T) was established in the Gaza Strip. Its aim was to eradicate all Jewish people and establish a continuous state from Iraq to the Mediterranean Sea.

Interestingly, at the same time Yasser Arafat held a PLO National council summit. The outcome was a declaration that the PLO now accepted Israel's right to exist and renounced terrorism. It later also declared the state of Palestine, and proclaimed that they were a 'government in exile!

In 1987, there was a collision between an Israeli military truck and a car carrying four Palestinian workers, who all died. Palestinian Arabs believed that this was a deliberate act by the soldiers as a reprisal for the killing of an Israeli in Gaza. This led to a concerted period of violent uprisings, riots, civil strikes and refusal to pay taxes. Israel reacted with suppression and lethal force, which was criticised as harsh and disproportionate by many international states. It lasted for six years.

## ISRAEL IN NEGOTIATION

The first Intifada presented the PLO with the opportunity to gain increasing political legitimacy on the world forum. The world had begun to to listen to their cause.  The level that this was achieved, was due to its leader, Yasser Arafat having convinced its national council to officially recognise Israel's right to exist, and call for a two-state solution where the original 1948 borders would be recognised.

# THE OSLO ACCORD

In 1993, Israel and the PLO Conducted secret negotiations, with the assistance of the US government. They became known as the Oslo Accords. The accords concluded that the territory in the Land would be divided into A, B and C categories.

**A- Palestinian territories under their administrative control.**

**B- mixed control**

**C- Israeli controlled areas.**

## IMPORTANT ASPECTS OF THE AGREEMENT

**Israel was required to construct a land border around the Gaza Strip. However, they would maintain control of the Airspace and waters. The PLO. became the Palestinian Authority with its Capital being set up in Ramallah. Its area of control was the West Bank and Gaza.**

The intension was that this would eventually lead to a two-state solution. Jerusalem stayed under Israel's control, but it is also claimed by the Palestinians *(Muslim majority)* to be theirs. *(Interestingly, Jerusalem is mentioned 806 times in the Bible, and 0 times in the Quran)*

As a response, billions of dollars of financial support and aid were poured into the newly created Palestinian territory towards infrastructure development and growth. It was said that the Gaza Strip had the potential to become the Singapore of the Middle East.

Despite these agreements, the implementation did not go smoothly causing the progress to halt, leading to yet again, more violence. There were several factors that possibly contributed to the fallout.

1 The different areas of control were not physically connected to each other, because Jewish territory divided them.

2 Israeli settlers continued to set up settlements beyond the 1967 boundaries. Currently there are over 100 communities that are separated by walls and military checkpoints.

3 Ariel Sharon visited the Temple mount in September 2, which the Palestinians stated was provoking the Palestinian Arab community.

## 2000 NEGOTIATIONS

Ehud Barak who was Prime minister in 2000, sought to re-initiate peace talks with the PLO, using the U.S. as a mediator. He brought to the table the offer of complete autonomy of the West Bank and Gaza. Essentially a two-state solution.
Unfortunately, the summit failed to reach a successful conclusion.

Both the U.S. and Israel lay the blame for failure at Arafat's feet, who it is said wanted as many concessions as possible without wanting peace. A key negotiator wrote that Arafat only really wanted a single Arab state, and not two adjacent states.

What could have been the end of conflict in the region was followed by the 2nd Palestinian Intifada, which was more brutal than the first. The consequence of this was that in 2002, the Israeli's built barriers and walls around West Bank, which were now under the control of the Palestinian Authority.

## ISRAEL WITHDRAWS FROM GAZA

In 2005, Israel made the unilateral decision to completely remove all Jewish presence from the Gaza area, handing over 21 established Israeli communities. The action caused a lot of heartache as many Israeli's were displaced, lost their homes, communities and livelihoods. Sadly, most of these communities no longer exist and were utterly destroyed within days by Gazan occupants.

The incorporated areas now came under the full control of the Palestinian Authority, with israel strengthening the border barrier.

Despite this disengagement by Israel, all was not well in Gaza. The controlling Palestinian Authority were accused of corruption and mis-management.

In 2006, Palestinian legislative elections were held. The Gazan's used their vote to speak out by choosing to elect the political wing of Hamas to take control.

Soon in-fighting ensued between Fatah and Hamas because neither of them wanted to share power. A short but bloody battle commenced in 2007, within the Gaza Strip, which eventually saw Hamas gaining outright authority over Gaza.

Now the Palestinians were divided both geographically and politically. For the past 15 years neither have held democratic elections again within the areas under their control.

In many ways, Israel has benefited from the division between the two Palestinian regions, and their ineptness and corruption.

In Gaza, Hamas proceeded to establish an Islamist rule and began using foreign aid to stockpile weapons, create tunnels and train military to further their aims of wiping out Israel. They control all aspects of governance, health and welfare, social development and infrastructure.

Since 2007, Hamas have indiscriminately fired thousands of rockets and carried out deadly attacks. They now boast of having 500km of tunnels, with hidden entrances in houses, mosques, schools and other public buildings. Yet, a large percentage of the population live below the poverty line, despite billions of pounds of aid.

Over these years, Hama's control has affected the attitude, mind set and environment of the Palestinian society. Many have from a very young age been trained and indoctrinated with the same spirit as Hamas'.
It is destructive, violent, and full of hate.

It takes an extreme level of pernicious brainwashing for individuals to commit the kind of heinous murderous acts that took place on 7th October 2023. When the perpetrators call their parents to inform them of what they have just done, and are praised for their actions, this cannot be considered as normal thinking, and shows that it is a generational problem.

Israel, completely aware of Hamas' aims, have regularly strengthened the border between them and the Gaza strip, only permitting access for humanitarian supplies through their checkpoint. Egypt also blocked their checkpoint too in the south, so that Gazans could not enter Egypt.

What initially was considered in the Oslo Accord as a potential international border, has become a concrete barrier built by Israel and Egypt to protect their territories against their actions. During the same period, there have been four significant battles between Hamas and Israel. Between 2005-2008 no less than 3,900 rockets were fired into Israel, with Israel reciprocating.

In December 2008 Israel launched a full-scale offensive against Hamas that lasted for three weeks, seeking to destroy their stockpile of weapons and underground tunnels.

Again, in Summer 2014, Palestinian unrest led to Hamas firing nearly 3,000 rockets into Israel. Israel responded with another air and ground offensive in Gaza. A cease-fire was brokered by Egypt. The Palestinian Authority declared that it would no longer recognise or abide with the Oslo Accords.

Moving on to 2018, Israel sought to undertake a covert operation, but were found out and Hamas responded by shelling Israel with hundreds of rockets. Israel then proceeded to fire back. It lasted for several days. Again, Israel was accused by the international community of committing a disproportionate response.

Between 2018-2023, there has been continual unrest throughout the West Bank, Jerusalem and Gaza. The cause of the disquiet has varied, ranging from individual attacks by both Palestinians and Israeli settlers, skirmishes on the Temple mount along with sporadic shelling from the Gaza Strip into Israel. In reality, it is all part of the long-term hatred and ownership of the land.

One particular example, was the removal of Palestinian residents from an East Jerusalem community, which owned originally by Sephardic Jews in the 19th century. Israel's laws allow Jews to file claims for property owned prior to 1948, but they reject any Palestinian claims for property that they owned prior to 1948, within the state Israel. Many would see this as evidence of Israeli apartheid.

In recent years Israel has faced internal political uncertainty, which has led to five snap elections in four years. This is largely due to shifting political and ethical opinions within Jewish society. The progress they have made for a young nation has been incredible, but as we have seen, they have also faced great opposition. Most citizens are fiercely nationalistic, but are tired of the conflicts and don't want the next generation to have to deal with the same problems. The result has been a rise in liberal inclinations, which has led to demonstrations and a polarisation of politics. At the age of 75, Israel is striving to find its Identity.

# HISTORICAL ASSESSMENTS

Following our brief examination of the historical events, it is possible to arrive at some initial observations.

## DOES ISRAEL HAVE A RIGHT TO THE LAND?
a) The Palestinian assertion that they are descendants of the Philistines, the original natives of the land that Israel overthrew, is not backed up by any evidence on both accounts.

History would record that the Philistines originated from the region of Crete and were considered the Vikings of the Mediterranean. It is evident though, that following Hadrian's expulsion of the Jews and the later rise of Islam, the region of Palestine became mainly populated by Arab people. However, it largely remained undeveloped apart from the major towns.

On the other side of the spectrum, there is considerable archeological and historical evidence to support Israel's claim to the land, both from an indigenous, moral and religious standpoint. In fact, it goes back to around 4,000 years.

Since their mass expulsion by Hadrian in 138AD, the Jewish people have never really fitted into any particular other geographical location or not faced repeatedly some form of exclusion, persecution and ghettoization. While other people groups have faced similar issues, the consistency of their plight has been unique.

Even in the early 20th century, recognition of their long association with the land was accepted. From the earliest days of the British Mandate, local coins were minted with text in English, Arabic and Hebrew. It should be noted that at the end of the of the Hebrew text in brackets is included ( י״א ), signifying, Eretz Israel - The land of Israel.

Long before the Holocaust, numerous western powers began to perceive the predicament of the Jews and listened to their cries to be restored to what they have always considered their homeland. It cannot be ignored that acknowledgments like the British Balfour Agreement (1917), and the League of Nations

San Remo Resolution (1920), which was ratified by the 51 member states in 1922, were a clear recognition and response to their understanding of the indigenous rights of the Jews. They also believed that recreating an independent Jewish State in that geographical location would not violate the rights of the existing inhabitants, albeit not potentially being without some complications. History shows that since 138AD, the area had always been incorporated into a larger region by successive powers, and there never existed an independent state of Palestine.

In spite of Arab protests against a Jewish state, the legal rights of the Jews to establish the autonomous State of Israel, was confirmed by the United Nations Resolution 181 in 1947. None of this can be ignored. It was always the hope that the Trans-Jordan Arab State and Israel could live in peace side by side, with both enjoying unconstrained freedom and democracy. However, as we have seen this has not proved to be the case.

We will cover more on this subject in Part 4, when discussing the biblical perspective.

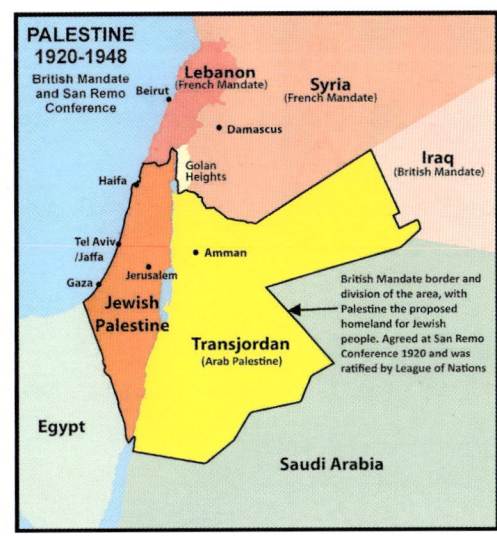

## ISRAEL'S OCCUPATION OF THE WEST BANK AND GAZA

a) Regarding Israel's illegitimate occupation of the West Bank and Gaza for the past 75 years, evidence shows that this is not as simple as people make out. In 1947, the United Nations earmarked two distinct and independent parcels of land for the state of Israel and Trans-Jordan Arabs. Israel accepted this, and proceeded to establish their new State. The moment they did so, the Arab nations attacked them. As we have seen, Israel overcame, and only claimed the land that the United Nations had granted them.

Between 1947-67, the West Bank and Gaza were under the direct control of neighbouring Arab nations. Egypt controlled the Gaza Strip and Jordan the West Bank. At no time did either of them consider those geographical areas the property of a specific Arab people group known as 'Palestinians'.  Nor did they seek to set up an independent Palestinian State.

Israel's control of these two areas was only as a result of them being attacked on numerous occasions by Egypt, Syria and Jordan. Their 'occupation' of these territories therefore came about as a defence, and not by their own predatory motives.

In subsequent negotiations neither Jordan or Egypt wanted the return of these regions. It was only then that the mention of a specific Palestinian people group was brought to the fore. Prior to this, it was considered as part of a wider argument regarding Israel's existence in the Middle East region.

Again, on numerous occasions Israel during negotiations, has offered the West Bank and Gaza to the Palestinian people, for their oversight and  independent control. In 2005, they even unilaterally withdrew all Jewish presence from Gaza.

Since then, the Palestinians have had the finance, international support and means to create that independence.  While there is poverty among the Palestinian people who reside there, there also exists considerable wealth and affluent areas too. It is a misconception that Israel has caused it to become 'an open prison'.

It would be true to say that Israel's control of these territories has been fraught with danger, causing much hurt and damage on both sides. Neither of the people groups have wanted integration. Israel see their military presence in certain areas of the West Bank as self defence, while the Palestinian Arabs see it as illegitimate occupation, especially with the increasing presence of Jewish settlers. While no one can deny that there were numerous Jewish communities existent within the West Bank area prior to 1948, it is true though that Israel has permitted a significant number to rise up in more recent years on land that has laid dormant for centuries. This has increased tensions between the two groups.

b) Israel's management of the West Bank has led to many of their opponents claiming that there now exists an apartheid state. Certainly, for those who live within the Israeli borders (see the Oslo accord agreement), and choose not to become a part of the Israeli State, or

who live under the Palestinian Authority, there are different rules. This is no different for any other democratic nation.

Interesting, ask a majority of Israeli Arabs who are members of Israel, if it is an apartheid state, they will respond that it is not. Both Jew and Arab have equal rights. They can own land, vote in the national and local elections, be members of parliament, be a judge on the Supreme Court, a police officer or a local Mayor; all serve in the army side by side. In fact it is frequently commented on, that Israel is the only real democracy within the Middle East. This is not to suggest that there are no internal issues or differences of opinion, but surely, that is the same everywhere, in every democracy!

# 2023 HAMAS ATTACK ON ISRAEL

On the 7th October 2023, Hamas conducted a ferocious, cold and calculated attack on Israeli communities close to the Gaza border. In the event over 1200 people were brutally and sadistically murdered, the majority of them being civilians of all ages. The day that Hamas launched the attack would have marked the 50th anniversary of the Yom Kippur war.

Israel and most of the world were stunned and horrified at what unfolded. Questions are being asked how could Israel have been so unprepared or lack prior intelligence to this event. Their response has been to organise a full scale war on Gaza with the intention to eliminate Hamas once and for all. Initially many world authorities have supported Israel's right to defend themselves, but this will not last.

The Palestinian people and certain Arab/Muslim nations, for the most part, have refused to condemn Hamas for their terrorist actions, choosing instead to blame Israel for causing oppression in the first place.

One aspect that cannot possibly be ignored is the reporting by the Media. At first they too focussed on the horrific acts committed by Hamas, however, once Israel embarked on a military response, the manner in which many have chosen to disseminate the information has changed. The focus now appears to be on the plight of the Palestinian people living in Gaza. This is not to say that they are unimportant, they are not. There is also a need to be mindful of how Israel acts, and the methods that it uses, in its attempt to remove Hamas (this will be discussed in Part Four). However, Hamas being a terrorist movement, uses modern media to spread disinformation and propaganda to divert away from their own oppressive acts against the Gazan people. It serves their purposes to have western media outlets and the masses blame Israel.

Since the attack, Hamas has released a document titled 'Our Narrative, Operation Al-Aqsa Flood'. The paper explains their reasons for the attack, which they perceive as defensive. It is claimed that their fighters only had military objectives, and no atrocities were committed against women and children, although accidents may have occurred. Furthermore, they refute being antisemitic, only anti-Zionist.

The narrative does not truthfully reflect what actually occurred that day. Honour and truth are not found in words printed in a glossy document, but in right actions and deeds.

Jeremiah 17:9

*The heart is deceitful above all things, and desperately sick; who can understand it?*

Equally, Israel is not above using modern media to spread disinformation as well.

We can see though, how quickly the world chooses to overlook the vile atrocities perpetrated against Israel in favour of criticising their response. The level of criticism and public demonstration, is in itself curious and displays an element of hypocrisy, and one has to wonder if there is potentially a disingenuous agenda behind it. This thought is aired because of the lack of similar responses towards the atrocities perpetrated against the Yemeni people, the Kurdish people and the Syrian's, in recent times.

Part of the problem for this could be, that generally speaking, the media and politicians only see and understand the Middle East issue as humanitarian/political/geographical struggle, and completely fail to see and understand an underlying spiritual battle. They are either totally blind or choose to reject a Biblical narrative being played out, and, of course, its final outcome. As soon as the phrase 'Biblical perspective', is ever mentioned, they start thinking of extreme fundamentalism.

As Christians, we cannot afford to be influenced by this kind of thinking, and must take time consider the spiritual perspective alongside the human one. If we fail to do so, then trying to navigate a way through this dilemma will be like going on a journey with only half a map.

We will now move on to the final section of this study, which will examine how we might respond from a spiritual perspective, that seeks to be both balanced and biblical.

> "As long as we continue to search for enemies anywhere but inside ourselves, there will always be a Middle East problem."

*Mosab Hassan Yousef*

# INTRODUCTION

7th October 2023, for the Jewish people was part of twenty-four hour period that celebrated the completion of the festival of Sukkot. Falling on a Shabbat made it a double blessing, and it would have incorporated two elements; Shemini Atzeret and Simchat Torah.

In Hebrew atzeret is associated with 'assembly', but it can also find its root in the word atzor, which means to 'stop' or 'wait'. Its application for this day, would then be to pause for reflection before moving forward. Many also choose it as time for Yizkor, the remembering of those who have passed away. Simchat Torah, brings the annual cycle of the reading of the Torah to a completion, only for it to commence again. It is a day that normally ends with dancing and the celebratory carrying of the Torah scroll.

Little did Jewish people in Israel know how deadly, vicious and demonic that day would turn out to be, concluding with a great deal of mourning for those who lost their lives in such a devastating manner. There would be no room for dancing and celebration.

On the flipside, there were many Palestinian people who lived in Gaza and the West Bank jumping and shouting for joy that day over the atrocities caused. For them it was a day of payback in their struggle for freedom against Israeli people.

The Middle-East conflict has once again been brought to the fore with diverse opinions and opposing viewpoints being aired.

For some, it is the struggle for freedom for the Palestinian people, against the oppressive and apartheid regime of modern state of Israel. For others, it is the ongoing struggle of the Israeli people to re-establish themselves in their ancient homeland, in the face of violent opposition from neighbouring Arab nations.

Then there are those who believe in Israel's spiritual right to the land, and that this is part of an ongoing spiritual battle that must be played out in order to fulfil the purposes of God. It should be noted that there are those in this latter group who, while acknowledging Israel's biblical right to the land, are uncomfortable with the severity of Israel's response.

# INITIAL THOUGHTS

## ISRAEL'S RIGHT TO THE LAND

From a historical position there is a great deal of evidence to support Israel's claim to be restored to the land, both from an indigenous standpoint and a moral stance. This is even before we consider the growing archaeological evidence, which is extremely compelling.

It would be inaccurate to claim that the ancient Philistines were the original inhabitants of the land, who Israel later overtook, since they came from Crete and were considered, for centuries, the Vikings of the Mediterranean. Hadrian later renaming Judea, Syria Palestina in the early 2nd Century, would be like kicking out today's Jews from the land, and renaming modern Israel, Hitlerana!

## ISRAEL'S SEPARATION FROM THE LAND

Considering that Jews have been exiled from Palestine for the past 1800 years and relocated to other countries, it would be important to consider their right to return. According to many, they should now be considerd as non-indigenous Judeans, who belong to the communities in which they settled.

If this is the case, one would ask, how does Israel fare alongside the Tibetans and North American Native Indians? Both have suffered persecution and forced diaspora. If they were granted by the world powers, the right to resettle into their native land and restore their independence, would they be reclassified several years later as colonial settlers?

It is interesting, that many who would seemingly champion their rights as indigenous people and campaign against their unfair treatment and the right to return, would deny Israel the same entitlement.

Despite being exiled, the Jews throughout the world have genetically, historically, theologically and culturally maintained their distinct identity. Often their failure to assimilate, has precluded them the right to own land, denied equal rights, maligned, persecuted and even killed.
Even many of their practices still point to a reminder of their connection with the land. Below are just a couple of examples:

> I. They pray towards Jerusalem at Passover they always say, "Next Year in Jerusalem", meaning God grant us the ability to celebrate this feast next year back in our homeland, Judea.

> ii. When every Jewish couple crush a glass at their wedding ceremony, they are reminding themselves of the destruction of the Jewish Temple in Jerusalem.

The question remains, how many generations does it take for them to be denied the right to return?

As Christians, to arrive at an informed answer to this question, it would be necessary for us to consider the theological aspect of the Jewish argument of the right to return.

The purpose of this section of the document will be to do precisely that.

## THEOLOGICAL QUESTIONS

Theologically there are so many questions and different pathways that we could explore, and each one could bear great relevance for our faith. It would be correct to briefly mention a number of them before our main topic, but would no doubt require further in-depth personal study to do them justice.

**a) Why did this attack occur, and what is the history of the conflict between Israel and Palestine?**
Many people would just refer to the past 75

years, since modern Israel became a nation. Yet, from a biblical perspective, as we have seen, one would have to start with the book of Genesis and the story of God's eternal promise to provide Abraham and his descendants with a specific parcel of land. Abraham who was aged and at that time childless, went on to have two sons, one with his wife's servant and another later on with his elderly wife. Many would consider this is where all the problems began.  As mentioned in our first chapter, Abraham's journey of faith was not always smooth and like most of us he had moments when he got things seriously wrong. Having a child with Sarah's handmaid, could be considered one of them.

**b) The question regarding the oppression of the Palestinian people by Israel.**
Considerable attention has been paid to this subject within the public arena in recent days. How we treat one another is an important biblical aspect.

Leviticus 19:33, clearly states that Israel has a responsibility to care for all who live in the land and treat them correctly.

*When a stranger sojourns with you in your land, you shall not do him wrong.*

Are they oppressing or defending? There is no secret about the suffering of the Jewish people themselves, and from the outset of their independence, they have faced deadly opposition from surrounding Arab states.  We know that they have suffered too throughout the whole of their history at the hands of gentile nations. We need to be mindful of why the world is so quick to attack them, malign them, persecute them, accuse them, even when they are seeking to defend themselves.

What is the spiritual significance associated with this?

**c) Do Israel have a right to defend themselves and what levels may be deemed correct and permissible?**
Included in this the question is a biblical perspective on the just war theory.

Is it correct to hold the opinion that war is despicable, but under certain conditions it can be both spiritually and ethically justified?

The Apostle Paul in Romans 13:1-5, states that those who violently attack governing authorities will face, not only the wrath of those in charge, but God too.

*"Let every person be subject to the governing authorities. For there is no authority except from God, and those that exist have been instituted by God. Therefore whoever resists the authorities resists what God has appointed, and those who resist will incur judgment. For rulers are not a terror to good conduct, but to bad. Would you have no fear of the one who is in authority? Then do what is good, and you will receive his approval, for he is God's servant for your good. But if you do wrong, be afraid, for he does not bear the sword in vain. For he is the servant of God, an avenger who carries out God's wrath on the wrongdoer. Therefore one must be in subjection, not only to avoid God's wrath but also for the sake of conscience."*

## Likewise, the Apostle Peter who also writes in 1 Peter 2:13–25

*"Submit yourselves for the Lord's sake to every authority instituted among men: whether to the king, as the supreme authority, or to the governors, who are sent by him to punish those who do wrong and to commend those who do right. For it is God's will that by doing good you should silence the ignorant talk of foolish men."*

Interestingly, one can seem to arrive at completely opposing views when considering the meaning of these verses. The first would support the idea of Christian pacifism, as we are advised to live orderly and obedient lives, even when we do not agree with the actions of governments and authorities, because they have been appointed by God. As an alternative, some would argue that, while we may not individually retaliate with violence against what we perceive as wrong, but trust God who will avenge for us (read Romans 12). God has empowered Kings, supreme rulers and governors, to execute that vengeance as His agents.

For every believer there is a tension between fighting against evil and loving our enemy. Rather than taking part in worldly affairs, should we seek out the way of love, thereby seemingly allowing evil to reign, or should we actively support a 'just war' when initiated by those in authority? Is it possible for there to be a middle ground?

## d) What leads them to commit acts of extreme violence and unbelievable horror on other people?

The atrocities of Hamas on 7th October have shown yet again, the wickedness in the hearts of men and women, who reject the love of God.

That day was surely one of the worst examples, not only because of the particular acts committed, but the glee with which they did those things to all ages. It would not be right though to provide specific details of those acts in this document, but they were wicked and monstrous.

King Solomon in his book of Proverbs wrote;

*Be not envious of evil men, nor desire to be with them, for their hearts devise violence, and their lips talk of trouble. Proverbs 24:1-2.*

*Where there is no prophetic vision the people cast off restraint, but blessed is he who keeps the law. Proverbs 29:18.*

The question of evil is of huge significance regardless of whether we are a theist or an atheist. Neither one can contest that acts of malicious intent are carried out everyday. What people do contest though, is the origin and source of why people act in this way. For Christians the answer lies in the doctrine of evil and the presence of satan. Its root or origin comes from willful opposition to God and a misuse of freewill.

Others would observe that the 'problem of evil', is actually an argument against the existence of God. The judgement of whether an individual's actions can be considered as right or wrong, can only be assessed by what the majority would set as an agreed standard of correct behaviour. So an individual or act, can only be condemned as wrongful when measured against a prior standard. C.S. Lewis, in his book Mere Christianity, explained this argument as follows:

*"A man does not call a line crooked unless he has some idea of a straight line."*

The problem arises in defining acts of atrocity in such a way, when one group of people differ on what is morally and ethically acceptable and what is not. Whose definition of right and wrong is the correct one?

A question that Nietzsche asked in his book, Genealogy of Morality, *'are the constructs of good and evil, a symptom of the distress, impoverishment, and degeneration of Human Life?'*

When it comes to the conflict between Israel and Palestine, there are those who would consider that the acts perpetrated by Hamas were simply an unsuppressed response to Israel's unjust suppression. While not openly justifying what took place, they would overlook such acts of violence, in favour of condemning Israel's response as disproportionate.

As Christians, can we agree with this kind of argument?

Conversely, there are those who would assert that what took place on October 7th, provides evidence of a 'systematic evil and hateful presence' which exists within Gazan society, as a result of methodical radicalisation. Until that indoctrination and those who teach it are removed, such violence will continue.

Again, as Christians, can we support this kind of argument? If this is true, how do we eradicate this evil?

Is there an alternative opinion, that views the actions of both parties to be a symptom of a fallen nature?

If this is the case, what should our practical response be? Or should we choose not to get involved or express an opinion?

**e) What should be our response to the masses who demonstrate, chanting 'from the river to the sea', and 'free Palestine'?**

This statement finds its roots in Islam. It refers to the presence of Jewish people in the geographical location. The sea represents the Mediterranean, and the river is either the River Jordan or the Euphrates. One takes their preference! Either way, it suggests that there will not be peace or freedom for the Palestinian people, until all Jewish people are removed from the land.

There follows also, a popular Arabic proverb which is frequently quoted in support of the Palestinian struggle, 'After Saturday comes Sunday'. (Meaning first we will deal with the Saturday people - Jews, then we will deal with the Sunday people - Christians). Its conclusion is the genocide of all Jewish people, leading to the establishment of a caliphate worldwide, with the death of all who oppose it!

There is evidence that many in the West have absorbed this narrative into there own concerns for the hostilities, potentially having no or little understanding of the full meaning of these chants; and that if carried out, it could lead to their own future subjugation and the possible death of many who choose not bow the knee to this particular ideology of Islam.

There are many who call themselves Christians, and have willingly participated in demonstrations and publically joined in with those chants.
Are we right to join these demonstrations knowing that majority support the sentiments previously spoken of. And is the calling for the removal of the Jewish people from the land, one that we can agree with theologically?

In 2 Corinthians 4:1-6, and 2 Timothy 2:1-13, the Apostle Paul expressed, that, God has called us to promote His message above everything else. We are not to involve ourselves in anything that we might be ashamed of or would bring contention to the gospel. The world does not believe what the Bible teaches nor accepts the message of Jesus because, *'the god of this world has confused their minds'.*
Do we need to be careful who we align with, and what we align with?
How important is it for the Church to provide biblical teaching on these subjects?

**f) The influence of false religion.**
As Christians, we have to accept that different world views will come into contention with biblical teaching. We need to be mindful how false religion can be a powerful weapon of satan.
It is also important to consider the effect that alternative religious views can have on the Church when they are allowed to permeate its thinking. It is a spiritual tactic of satan in order to cause its destruction.

While individual churches may be maintaining Godly principles, a large section of the wider Church have capitulated to outside influences and appear to be in spiritual trouble. Many now bow the knee to popular opinion and worldly lifestyles.

War is not just raging in the physical realm it is taking place in the spiritual too. It is a war for our souls and minds; for God's Church, for the integrity and truth of His word, and for the identity of and purposes for Israel. It may seem a strong statement, but if we do not already see this, maybe, we need to remove our spiritual blinkers.

Matthew 7:15

*"Beware of false prophets, who come to you in sheep's clothing but inwardly are ravenous wolves."*

1 Timothy 4:1

*"Now the Spirit expressly says that in later times some will depart from the faith by devoting themselves to deceitful spirits and teachings of demons,"*

2 Timothy 4:2

*"For the time will come when people will not put up with sound doctrine. Instead, to suit their own desires, they will gather around them a great number of teachers to say what their itching ears want to hear. They will turn their ears away from the truth and turn aside to myths."*

Galatians 1:8–9

*But even if we or an angel from heaven should preach to you a gospel contrary to the one we preached to you, let him be accursed. As we have said before, so now I say again: If anyone is preaching to you a gospel contrary to the one you received, rlet him be accursed.*

Is it possible that the Church is now at a crossroads?
Some will turn one way - other's another; and out of it will come two churches.

a) A larger, false one that capitulates to world opinions.

b) A smaller, true one, but will be far more powerful and Holy Spirit led which will maintain biblical teaching.
Alongside other issues, Israel will be at the heart of which way we choose.

**g) Do current events in the Middle East indicate that we are entering the end times?**
There are those who consider that we are very close to what the Bible calls 'the end times', a period that precedes the return of Jesus Christ. They would point to biblical references

which indicate that the conflict between Israel and the Arabs will not stop until the battle of Armageddon – where God judges the nations for their actions against Israel.

This is a subject on its own, and one which FOI has discussed at length in a separate study.

## DEVELOPING A THEOLOGICAL PERSPECTIVE

Despite the importance of the previous subjects, they do not necessarily inform us as to the level of Israel's and the land's theological significance. Without this understanding we will be unable to arrive at our goal of building a sound theological perspective.

## OUR APPROACH

In 1970, the business theorist, Chris Argyris published a model of thinking which he called 'The ladder of Inference'. It outlines a process of thinking that enables someone to arrive at a final and informed conclusion. The theory is, that by analysing data and facts in an unbiased manner, it helps to prevent one from jumping to conclusions.

Educators refer to this as inductive thinking, which is based on collecting all the information before reaching a conclusion, as opposed to deductive thinking which works with limited information to form a decision and then gathers supporting evidence as you proceed.

When considering the Middle East dilemma from both a historical and theological perspective, the inductive approach is extremely relevant. Employing this model will enable us to glean significant information in order to form a biblical perspective. Our approach will be to conduct an overview of the biblical story and hopefully, as we do so, a clear picture will emerge and the pieces will fall into place. From there we choose how we might reference it in the current Israeli – Palestine conflict. We will cover the following subjects:

Who owns the land?

Is the land special and does God have a purpose for it?

How are the people of Israel involved and are they special?

Why has the land caused so many troubles?

Why is it that the world powers can never sort this out?

What should be Israel's response?

What should the Church's response be?

## WHO OWNS THE LAND?

The preoccupying question for many today regarding the conflict, revolves around - who owns the land? This is an important question, so we will start with 'WHO', which will lead onto the 'WHY'.

The Palestinian Arabs contend that the land is theirs, and that they are a persecuted people subjugated by a foreign enemy who have sought to supplant them. Many of them in fact, would now even claim that they are direct descendants of the Canaanites. Yet again, there is no evidence to back this up, despite many Muslim Arab nations and 'scholars' supporting this claim.

Now, the Jewish people would point out that along with the historical and biblical evidence, it was they who were subjugated for hundreds of years, then cruelly displaced and forced to wander homeless through this world for nearly 2,000 years. In those intervening years, they were scorned, maligned, abused and massacred to near extinction.

In the early 20th century, the western powers acknowledged the pleas of the Jewish people to be permitted to restore the State of Israel. As we have seen in the earlier chapters of this study, plans were set afoot to make this a reality.  It was not until the Holocaust was made known following WW2, that many of the wider world powers finally took notice of their plight too, and supported their right to return and re-establish the State of Israel.

Interestingly, there are even verses in the Quaran that confirm the people of Israel's (Jewish people), ancient association with the land. Here are just a couple.

*Quaran Surah 5:20-21- it states that Allah gave Israel the land.*

*Surah Al-Dukhan 44:32 – the children of Israel are inheritors of the land.*

## WHAT DOES THE BIBLE SAY?

Despite the arguments, it is possible that neither of them owns the land. In reading the Old and New Testaments, we learn a different story, which should be taken into account as we respond to the current situation. Scripture explains not only who owns the land, but also its purpose, the reason for ongoing conflict, and the ultimate outcome. We will consider each one of these subjects in turn. Let's begin with the question of ownership.

Psalms 115:16, informs us that after God created the earth he gave it to man, so in a sense, we all own it collectively and have responsibility for its well being.

*The heavens are the LORD's heavens,*
*but the earth he has given to the children of man.*

However, we are also told that there is one particular part of the earth that God has chosen to claim for himself.

## Leviticus 25: 23

*The land must not be sold permanently, because the land is mine and you reside in my land as foreigners and strangers. Throughout the land that you hold as a possession, you must provide for the redemption of the land.*

We learn from this, that Israel is warned not to sell the land because it belongs to Him - they are its guests.

In Deuteronomy chapter 11, we are told that God cares for this strip of land and His eyes are always on it, watching what happens to It.

## Deuteronomy. 11:11- 12

*But the land you are crossing the Jordan to take possession of is a land of mountains and valleys that drinks rain from heaven. It is a land the LORD your God cares for; the eyes of the LORD your God are continually on it from the beginning of the year to its end.*

Read the prophet Joel and we discover that God is Jealous for this Land, and is mindful for the people who live in it, no matter who they are.

## Joel 2:18

*Then the LORD became jealous for His land and had pity on his people.*
*In Jeremiah we discover that He gets upset when people, especially the Jewish people abuse it.*

## Jeremiah 2:7

*And I brought you into a plentiful land to enjoy its fruits and its good things.*
*But when you came in, you defiled my land and made my heritage an abomination.*

It is important to understand that God will never let go of this land, because through it He has chosen to let the world witness His Holiness and glory.

Even in the last days the land still belongs to Him. He will allow the nations to invade Israel and come against the Jewish people, but He does not permit them to be destroyed, as the purpose is for the world to see His glory.

## Ezekiel 38:16

*You will come up against my people Israel, like a cloud covering the land. In the latter days I will bring you against my land, that the nations may know me, when through you, O Gog, I vindicate my holiness before their eyes.*

It is in the land that He will judge the nations for the way that they have treated his people Israel and divided His land among themselves.

Joel 3:2
*I will gather all the nations and bring them down to the Valley of Jehoshaphat. And I will enter into judgment with them there, on behalf of my people and*

*my heritage Israel, because they have scattered them among the nations and have divided up my land, . . . .*

Yes, He has given the world to mankind to manage, but there is a particular parcel of it that remains for his own purposes.

Those who think that it is theirs and fight over it, or have sought to divide it up or partition it, need to be mindful. They will face His wrath and His Judgement in the last days!

## WHAT ARE GOD'S PURPOSES FOR THE LAND?

So far we have learnt from the Old Testament, that God has chosen this particular portion of land for His purposes; which makes the area unique and special. But why?
To reveal the answer, we will have to take a journey through the biblical narratives, where we will unveil an epic and dramatic story. Here is where the 'big picture' will start to come into view, and we will rely heavily on scripture to help develop it.

### IT BEGINS WITH CREATION
Genesis. 1:1
*In the beginning God created the heavens and the earth.*

Genesis Chapter one, is a combination of historical fact and Jewish poetry which informs us of the beginnings of creation.  It is the story of a singular divine creator who designs and makes all things.   The Apostle Paul in Colossians 1:16-17, confirms this.

*For in him all things were created: things in heaven and on earth, visible and invisible, whether thrones or powers or rulers or authorities; all things have been created through him and for him.  He is before all things, and in him all things hold together.*

Reading the numerous passages throughout the bible, we discover that this divine being created two distinct kingdoms, each having unique natures with different kind of beings occupying them.

**First was the Kingdom of heaven**
It is the eternal dwelling place of God, and populated with an assortment of heavenly beings.

**Second came the Kingdom of earth.**
This is the dwelling place of humans and the animal kingdom.

There are two key Hebrew words that appear in the first chapter of Genesis which explain mankind's purpose. The first is Rada, which can be translated as 'rule', and the second is Kabash, which means 'to manage'.
Man has been given authority over the earth, but always in partnership with God and under His authority.

Mankind is not, and never will be the creator, but are created co-workers to develop and build an environment that displays the glory of God and reflects His attributes. Unlike the heavenly beings, mankind can fulfill this function on earth because God breathed the very breath of life into them and uniquely passed on many of His attributes.

In the beginning there was harmony, peace, co-operation and an order with everything being and functioning in its correct place.
The divine creator who is holy, blessed, sacred and righteous, created a world and a human being that is also holy, blessed, sacred and righteous.
*(This does not mean that the heavenly beings are not sentient also, they are, but in a different way and different realm).*

Ephesians 1:4.
*Even as he chose us in him before the foundation of the*

*world, that we should be holy and blameless before him. In love he predestined us for adoption to himself as sons through Jesus Christ, according to the purpose of his will, to the praise of his glorious grace, with which he has blessed us in the Beloved.*

## THE PARTNERSHIP WAS QUICKLY BROKEN

The biblical narratives inform us, that there was one who was a part of the first heavenly creation, who rebelled and sought to over throw God and take His place. We cannot be certain, but it would appear that he objected to the creation of mankind and the earth.

In the Bible, he is attributed various names – the serpent, ha satan (the accuser), the devil (supreme evil spirit), morning star, the anointed cherub, prince of darkness, lucifer, beelzebub (lord of dung).

Isaiah 14:12.

*How you have fallen from heaven, O morning star, son of the dawn! You have been cut down to the ground, O destroyer of nations. You said in your heart: "I will ascend to the heavens; I will raise my throne above the stars of God. I will sit on the mount of assembly, in the far reaches of the north. I will ascend above the tops of the clouds; I will make myself like the Most High."*

Ezekiel 28:12ff.

*'Thus says the Lord GOD: "You were the seal of perfection, Full of wisdom and perfect in beauty. You were in Eden, the garden of God; Every precious stone was your covering: The sardius, topaz, and diamond, beryl, onyx, and jasper, sapphire, turquoise, and emerald with gold.*

*The workmanship of your timbrels and pipes was prepared for you on the day you were created. "You were the anointed cherub who covers; I established you; you were on the holy mountain of God; you walked back and forth in the midst of fiery stones. You were perfect in your ways from the day you were created, till sin was found in you. "By the abundance of your trading you became filled with violence within, and you sinned; therefore, I cast you as a profane thing out of the mountain of God;*

Battle ensued, but he was eventually defeated, and kicked out of heaven along with those who fought alongside him.

From that moment on he made it his aim to

separate mankind from God, and then ruin and destroy any image and goodness of God within us and the world.

Revelation 12:7-9.

*Now war arose in heaven, Michael and his angels fighting against the dragon. And the dragon and his angels fought back, but he was defeated, and there was no longer any place for them in heaven. And the great dragon was thrown down, that ancient serpent, who is called the devil and Satan, the deceiver of the whole world—he was thrown down to the earth, and his angels were thrown down with him.*

In Genesis 3, we are told that man and woman quickly became beguiled by this supernatural being and fell under the power of his lies and deception. Their actions is called 'sin', and the event is now known as 'the Fall'.

In the creation story, sin is characterised by Adam and Eve no longer accepting God's order which He had initially put in place, choosing instead to live by an alternative order.

As a consequence of their actions, mankind began to look at the physical world to meet their needs that only a spiritual God could and should provide; but now cannot. Instead, mankind looks to a lower order of things, to meet only that which the higher order can; we are putting trust in and relying on a greedy, self seeking, inferior order.

Instead of life and dynamic growth, based upon peace, harmony, unity, trust and Love, we now have death destruction, disease, distrust, hate, bitterness, greed, envy, selfishness and perversion. This is because the vital cord between the divine creator and His creation (which is the life-blood) has been severed.

It is possible to liken this event, to satan having infected mankind with a powerful and destructive virus that has been passed down through every generation. Its aim is to eradicate the attributes of God in us and replace them with rebellion, hate, bitterness, violence, spite, envy, greed, anger, deception, division and murder.

The ultimate outcome is separation from God and mortality. This is reflected by the removal of Adam and Eve from the garden of Eden. All of mankind carry that original infection to this day. The bible has named this virus as sin.

If you take a flower out of the ground and sever it from its life blood it will continue to look alive. There are certain additives that you can put into the water to help maintain 'life', but its cells will breakdown and the death clock has begun to tick. For mankind, the countdown has begun. Death is inevitable.

Romans 3:23.

*For all have sinned and fall short of the glory of God.*

1 John 1:8.

*If we claim to be without sin, we deceive ourselves and the truth is not in us.*

Mark 7:20.

*He went on: "What comes out of a person is what defiles them. For it is from within, out of a person's heart, that evil thoughts come—sexual immorality, theft, murder, adultery, greed, malice, deceit, lewdness, envy, slander, arrogance and folly All these evils come from inside and defile a person."*

## WHAT ARE GOD'S PURPOSES FOR THE LAND?

The sinful nature within mankind has rendered us incapable of reconciling ourselves with God or of having the ability to eliminate the power of the virus within us. Adam and Eve's original sinful corruption has been passed down to all generations, corrupting our conscience, moral judgements, will, thought process and mortality.

Psalm 51:5.

*Surely I was sinful at birth, sinful from the time my mother conceived me.*

Psalm 14:3

*All have turned away, all have become corrupt; there is no one who does good, not even one.*

Ecclesiastes 7:20

*Surely there is not a righteous man on earth who does good and never sins.*

The Old Testament book of Job explains the dilemma and expresses the need for a mediator who can appeal on our behalf before God.

Job 9:32

*God is not a mortal like me, so I cannot argue with him or take him to trial. If only there were a mediator between us, someone who could bring us together.*

The words of Job actually echo the mind of God, who had already developed a plan to reclaim mankind and to set us free from the power of sin and its affects. He would accomplish this in two stages which requires a special and unique mediator.

God's mediator would be divine and a human descendant of Adam and Eve. He would possess the supernatural ability to destroy the power of sin in us, and then satan himself.

Using the analogy of the virus again, the antidote that provides restoration and healing for humanity, is present in the blood of the mediator, who freely sacrifices his life for our atonement.

Genesis 3:15

*"I will put enmity between you and the woman, and between your offspring and her offspring; he shall bruise your head, and you shall bruise his heel."*

Isaiah 7:14

*"Therefore the Lord Himself will give you a sign: Behold, a virgin will be with child and bear a son, and she will call His name Immanuel."*

## THE WORK OF THE MEDIATOR

This mediator has two functions, which he fulfils in two separate stages.

1. First, he comes to deal with the power of sin. This would be through a blood sacrifice. This is the work of the Suffering Messiah. He also teaches a different way of living, which would help us overcome the deplorable affects of sin in our lives.

## Isaiah 53:1ff.

*Who has believed our message and to whom has the arm of the LORD been revealed?*

*He grew up before him like a tender shoot, and like a root out of dry ground. He had no beauty or majesty to attract us to him, nothing in his appearance that we should desire him.*

*He was despised and rejected by mankind, a man of suffering, and familiar with pain.*

*Like one from whom people hide their faces he was despised, and we held him in low esteem.*

*Surely he took up our pain and bore our suffering, yet we considered him punished by God, stricken by him, and afflicted. But he was pierced for our transgressions, he was crushed for our iniquities; the punishment that brought us peace was on him, and by his wounds we are healed.*

*We all, like sheep, have gone astray, each of us has turned to our own way; and the LORD has laid on him the sin of us all.*

## Daniel 9:25-26

*Know therefore and understand that from the going out of the word to restore and build Jerusalem to the coming of an anointed one, a prince, there shall be seven weeks. Then for sixty-two weeks it shall be built again with squares and moat, but in a troubled time. And after the sixty-two weeks, an anointed one shall be cut off and shall have nothing. And the people of the prince who is to come shall destroy the city and the sanctuary.*

## Psalm 22: 16-18

*For dogs encompass me; a company of evildoers encircles me; they have pierced my hands and feet. I can count all my bones— they stare and gloat over me; they divide my garments among them, and for my clothing they cast lots.* **(The whole of Psalm 22 is associated with the suffering Messiah)**

## Zechariah 12:10

*"And I will pour out on the house of David and the inhabitants of Jerusalem a spirit of grace and pleas for mercy, so that, when they look on me, on him whom they have pierced, they shall mourn for him, as one mourns for an only child, and weep bitterly over him, as one weeps over a firstborn."*

## John 3:16

*"For God so loved the world, that he gave his only Son, that whoever believes in him should not perish but have eternal life."*

2. Second, having dealt with sin, he returns to deal with the one who put the virus in us. He

deals with satan. This is the Kingly Messiah.

## Isaiah 9:6-7

*For to us a child is born, to us a son is given; and the government shall be upon his shoulder, and his name shall be called Wonderful Counselor, Mighty God, Everlasting Father, Prince of Peace. Of the increase of his government and of peace there will be no end, on the throne of David and over his kingdom, to establish it and to uphold it with justice and with righteousness from this time forth and forevermore. The zeal of the LORD of hosts will do this.*

## Micah 5:2

*But you, O Bethlehem Ephrathah, who are too little to be among the clans of Judah, from you shall come forth for me one who is to be ruler in Israel, whose coming forth is from of old, from ancient days.*

## Psalm 110. A Psalm of David.

*The Lord says to my Lord: "Sit at my right hand, until I make your enemies your footstool." The Lord sends forth from Zion your mighty sceptre. Rule in the midst of your enemies!*

*Your people will offer themselves freely on the day of your power, in holy garments; from the womb of the morning, the dew of your youth will be yours.*

*The Lord has sworn and will not change his mind, "You are a priest forever after the order of Melchizedek." The Lord is at your right hand; he will shatter kings on the day of his wrath. ...*

## Zechariah 9:9

*Rejoice greatly, O daughter of Zion! Shout aloud, O daughter of Jerusalem! Behold, your king is coming to you; righteous and having salvation is he, humble and mounted on a donkey, on a colt, the foal of a donkey.*

## Jeremiah 23:5

*"Behold, the days are coming, declares the Lord, when I will raise up for David a righteous Branch, and he shall reign as king and deal wisely, and shall execute justice and righteousness in the land.*

## Revelation 1:7

*"Behold, he is coming with the clouds, and every eye will see him, even those who pierced him, and all tribes of the earth will wail on account of him. Even so. Amen.*

## Daniel 7:13-14

*"I saw in the night visions, and behold, with the clouds of heaven there came one like a son of man, and he came to the Ancient of Days and was presented before him. And to him was given dominion and glory and*

*a kingdom, that all peoples, nations, and languages should serve him; his dominion is an everlasting dominion, which shall not pass away, and his kingdom one that shall not be destroyed."*

Revelation 20:10

*And the devil who had deceived them was thrown into the lake of fire and sulfur, into which the beast and the false prophet had already been thrown. There they will be tormented day and night forever and ever.*

## WHO IS THIS PROMISED MEDIATOR?

Despite the biblical references outlining the work of the Messiah, the identity, specific nature and function of the Messiah is still debated among the different factions within Judaism.

There are those who accept the belief of a single Messiah. For them, he is a human, kingly Messiah who will bring victory over their human oppressors, but they would discount any notion of him suffering for sin. Others hold to a 'two Messiah' concept. Messiah Ben David, the final redeemer, and Messiah Ben Yossef (or Ephraim). He will come ahead of the final redeemer, and then later serve as his consul. Still, there are others, who would contend that the Messiah is not a single individual, but the nation of Israel itself who will usher in a 'Messianic Age'. All however, believe that he or this messianic age, is yet to come.

Throughout the ages, there are many who have proclaimed themselves to be the Jewish Messiah. There was one though, who came at the outset of the first century AD, who not only fulfilled 90% of the prophesies*, but also displayed the qualities and supernatural abilities to back up his claim, including resurrection from the dead. His name was Yeshua (Jesus).

*(*The other 10% refers to end time events.)*

During his time on earth, he had a significant impact and gathered many followers, some of the most notable ones, wrote comprehensive accounts of his life and ministry. Following his death, his adherents have grown globally to become the largest faith on earth. Despite this many Jewish people have chosen to reject him as their Messiah.

There are a number of reasons for this, but one particularly that stands out.
Both in Jesus' time and now, the Jewish people have only sought redemption from their human oppressors. They have never considered the need to be released from the power and effects of sin. This is because they reject the concept of original sin or that they are born sinful (regardless of Old Testament scriptures stating this to be the case, as we have shown). As a result, they believe that they can do this of their own ability by following the Torah. Yet, time and time again it has been shown that this is not possible. Even the most righteous of Rabbi's have never managed this.

*'All have sinned and fallen short of the glory of God'.*

It is not possible for sinful Jews to be their own sin bearers. They need someone beyond themselves, as do we all.

Their rejection of this has sought them to reinterpret scripture in a way that would meet their chosen preferences.

Once again, despite the overwhelming biblical evidence, they do not accept the idea of the Messiah dying for the sins of mankind or being a spiritual deliverer. Therefore, most modern Jews do not see the Messiah in the same way that Christians do, so the claims of the New Testament do not resonate with their worldview.

As Christians though, we believe that there is enough evidence and eyewitness accounts to show that Yeshua was and is the promised Messiah, both as the suffering servant and the coming King.

Acts 26:22-23

*But God has helped me to this very day; so I stand here and testify to small and great alike.*
*I am saying nothing beyond what the prophets and Moses said would happen— that the Messiah would suffer and, as the first to rise from the dead, would bring the message of light to his own people and to the Gentiles.*

## Romans 5:10

*For since our friendship with God was restored by the death of his Son while we were still his enemies, we will certainly be saved through the life of his Son.*

*So now we can rejoice in our wonderful new relationship with God because our Lord Jesus Christ has made us friends of God.*

## 2 Corinthians 5:18

*God has done it all! He sent Christ to make peace between himself and us, and he has given us the work of making peace between himself and others.*

## Galatians 4:4

*But when the fullness of time had come, God sent forth his Son, born of woman, born under the law.*

## 1 Timothy 1:15

*It is a trustworthy statement, deserving full acceptance, that Christ Jesus came into the world to save sinners, among whom I am foremost of all.*

## Titus 2:13

*while we look forward with hope to that wonderful day when the glory of our great God and Savior, Jesus Christ, will be revealed. He gave his life to free us from every kind of sin, to cleanse us, and to make us his very own people, totally committed to doing good deeds.*

## Matthew 26:64

*Jesus said to him, "You have said so. But I tell you, from now on you will see the Son of Man seated at the right hand of Power and coming on the clouds of heaven."*

## John 14:1-3

*"Let not your hearts be troubled. Believe in God; believe also in me. In my Father's house are many rooms. If it were not so, would I have told you that I go to prepare a place for you?*

*And if I go and prepare a place for you, I will come again and will take you to myself, that where I am you may be also.*

## Acts 1:10-11

*And while they were gazing into heaven as he went, behold, two men stood by them in white robes, and said, "Men of Galilee, why do you stand looking into heaven? This Jesus, who was taken up from you into heaven, will come in the same way as you saw him go into heaven."*

## Titus 2:13

*Waiting for our blessed hope, the appearing of the glory of our great God and Saviour Jesus Christ....*

**1 Thessalonians 4:13-18**

*But we do not want you to be uninformed, brothers, about those who are asleep, that you may not grieve as others do who have no hope. For since we believe that Jesus died and rose again, even so, through Jesus, God will bring with him those who have fallen asleep. For this we declare to you by a word from the Lord, that we who are alive, who are left until the coming of the Lord, will not precede those who have fallen asleep.*
*For the Lord himself will descend from heaven with a cry of command, with the voice of an archangel, and with the sound of the trumpet of God. And the dead in Christ will rise first. Then we who are alive, who are left, will be caught up together with them in the clouds to meet the Lord in the air, and so we will always be with the Lord ...*

**1 Thessalonians 5:2-3**

*Now may the God of peace himself sanctify you completely, and may your whole spirit and soul and body be kept blameless at the coming of our Lord Jesus Christ.*

# HOW IS GOD GOING TO FULFIL THIS PLAN?

## He would use a specific people group

The Bible informs us that in order to fulfil His plan of redemption, God would choose a specific people group, who He would then have live in the land, through which He has chosen to carry out His divine purposes.

By obeying the Torah, worshipping in the Temple, and presenting blood sacrifices as an offering for forgiveness, God creates and develops in them a sense of holy purpose, causing them to become a holy people living in a holy land. As long as He needed them to fulfil His divine mission, they would be His.

Through them the Mediator (who He called the Messiah, meaning saviour) would be born. It was the Jewish people who He selected for this purpose and placed them in the land of Canaan, preparing them for this event.

## Does this Make the Jewish People Special?

It is important to understand that on a

personal level, there is nothing to set Jewish people apart from any other individual. Everybody needs rescuing from the power of sin. In order to receive forgiveness of sin and re-establish a relationship with God, all people must accept God's chosen Messiah, recognise His Lordship, and that through His sacrificial death and subsequent resurrection will make us all sons and daughters of God.

As commented previously, we believe that there exists enough proof and eyewitness evidence to believe that Yeshua is God's Messiah. It was through His earthly life, death and resurrection that He fulfilled the first stage of His work as the suffering Messiah.

There are Christians who advocate that Jewish people can be saved without coming through Yeshua (it is called dual covenant theology), this is an incorrect assumption.

There are also those who see Jews as something special and place them on some kind of holy pedestal. This would be wrong too.
In Romans 3:23, the apostle Paul writes that

*'all have sinned all have fallen short of God's glory'.*

Later, in his letter to the Galatians, Paul confirms this lack of distinction.

Galatians 3:28

*There is neither Jew nor Greek, there is neither slave nor free, there is no male and female, for you are all one in Christ Jesus.*

However, while there is nothing unique about Jewish people on an individual level, there is something totally unique about Israel as a nation and a people, that is the difference! It is a divine corporate difference.

Genesis 15 & 17, speaks of God making a special covenant, that provides specific promises, blessings and curses to this people group. First through Abraham and then confirmed later through Moses in the book of Exodus. We covered this in the earlier chapters of our study.

Paul confirmed that God has no more or less love for a Jewish person than a Gentile. As a nation and a people, He does have a special love for Israel, and actually, also for the Arab people as well – both being children of Abraham (not as individuals, but as people groups - with different kind of blessings).

The Jewish people, were initially placed under a corporate and specific divine law, based on blessings, curses and animal sacrifice. This is called the Old Covenant or Old Testament.

## WHAT WAS THE PROCESS?

We conducted a survey of the process that God used in the first section, but we will do a quick recap.

a) God chose an individual – His name was Abram and was the first to be promised the land.

b) It continued through and the descendants became a family – Isaac and Jacob (later Israel).

c) Israel's children grew into a large family- they left the land for Egypt due to famine.

d) The family became the nation of Israel – they were brought back to the land to repossess it.

e) God instructed Israel to follow a stringent religious code and practice that involved blood sacrifice for the forgiveness of sins. It is known as the Torah Covenant. As a result of human sin, however, they failed to live up to this covenant, time and time again disobeying God and following their own path.

Romans 9:4-5

*who are Israelites, to whom belongs the adoption as sons, and the glory and the agreements and the giving of God's instructions and the temple service and the promises, whose are the fathers, and from whom is the Christ according to the flesh, who is over all, God blessed forever. Amen.*

Deuteronomy 7:6-8

*"For you are a people holy to the LORD your God. The LORD your God has chosen you out of all the peoples on the face of the earth to be his people, his treasured possession. The LORD did not set his affection on you and choose you because you were more numerous than other peoples, for you were the fewest of all peoples.*

*But it was because the LORD loved you and kept the promise he swore to your ancestors that he brought you out with a mighty hand and redeemed you from the land of slavery, from the power of Pharaoh king of Egypt."*

## Leviticus. 25: 23

*The land must not be sold permanently, because the land is mine and you reside in my land as foreigners and strangers. Throughout the land that you hold as a possession, you must provide for the redemption of the land.*

God's enemy continually seeks to thwart His plans. Satan has always had a brutal and relentless hatred for the Jewish people because he knows that they are chosen by God to be the conduit through which His salvation comes.

He has sought to do everything to prevent them from fulfilling God's purposes. Below are a few examples.

### a. Make them a rebellious people.

Psalm 78:40

*How often they rebelled against Him in the wilderness and grieved Him in the desert!*

## Nehemiah 9:16-31

*"But they, our fathers, acted arrogantly; They became stubborn and would not listen to Your commandments. "They refused to listen, And did not remember Your wondrous deeds which You had performed among them;..."*

### b. To make them want to be ordinary like other nations.

1 Sam. 8:4,20

*"appoint for us, then, a king to govern us, like other nations."*

God inform Israel through the prophet Samuel, that He was their king; nevertheless, the people refused to listen to Samuel. "No", they said. "We must have a king over us. Then we will be like all the other nations, with a king to judge us, to go out before us, and to fight our battles."

God gave them what they wished for, but it would eventually lead to division and their expulsion from the land.

## Ezekiel 20:32

*"What is in your mind shall never happen—the thought, 'Let us be like the nations, like the tribes of the countries, and worship wood and stone.'*

### c. To make them follow false gods.

Hosea 2:13

*"Israel served false gods, so I will punish her. She burned incense to those false gods. She dressed up—she put on her jewellery and nose ring. Then she went to her lovers and forgot me."*

### d. To do everything to remove them from the land.

2 Kings 17:23

*So the people of Israel were taken from their homeland into exile in Assyria, and they are still there.*

Psalm 83:2

*See how your enemies growl, how your foes rear their heads. With cunning they conspire against your people; they plot against those you cherish. "Come," they say, "let us destroy them as a nation, so that Israel's name is remembered no more."*

Luke 21:24

*They will fall by the edge of the sword and be led captive among all nations, and Jerusalem will be trampled underfoot by the Gentiles, until the times of the Gentiles are fulfilled.*

But God has promised to restore them and replant them into the land.

Jeremiah. 31:17

*So there is hope for your descendants," declares the LORD. "Your children will return to their own land.*

Jeremiah 16:14

*However, the days are coming," declares the LORD, "when it will no longer be said, 'As surely as the LORD lives, who brought the Israelites up out of Egypt,' but it will be said, 'As surely as the LORD lives, who brought the Israelites up out of the land of the north and out of all the countries where he had banished them.' For I will restore them to the land I gave their ancestors.*

Zechariah 12:2

*"I am going to make Jerusalem a cup that sends all the surrounding peoples reeling.Judah will be besieged as well as Jerusalem. On that day, when all the nations of the earth are gathered against her, I will make Jerusalem an immovable rock for all the nations. All who try to move it will injure themselves. "The LORD will save the dwellings of Judah first, so that the honour of the house of David and of Jerusalem's inhabitants may not be greater than that of Judah. On that day the LORD will shield those who live in Jerusalem, so that the feeblest among them will be like David, and the house of David*

*will be like God, like the angel of the LORD going before them. On that day I will set out to destroy all the nations that attack Jerusalem.*

### e. To destroy them.

Time and time again we have seen down through history that the Jewish people have been persecuted almost to extinction.

Satan has done everything to get them out of the way and separate them from the land, with the aim of stopping God's plans. But God is faithful and His purposes will not be thwarted, and he has always redeemed them, preserved them even if it is a small group.  And know this, He always will!

## GOD IS NOT FINISHED WITH ISRAEL

There are many, even in the Church who believe that God is finished with Israel and the Jewish people. This has affected Christian attitudes towards them. Apologetic writings as early as the second century depict antisemitic attitudes running through the Church. It is commonly believed that the Jewish people are now a cursed people because they have rejected Jesus as God's promised Messiah, and the Church has taken their place.

Despite this common opinion, it is important to consider if this is a true reflection of scripture.

It is true that Jesus is cited by the apostle John calling the 'Jews', sons of the devil, and not true sons of Abraham. John 8:39-44.

*You belong to your father, the devil, and you want to carry out your father's desires. He was a murderer from the beginning, not holding to the truth, for there is no truth in him. When he lies, he speaks his native language, for he is a liar and the father of lies.*

As always, context is important, and these verses are part of a wider passage outlining a discussion that Jesus was having with a specific group of religious Pharisees (see John 8:13).

CONFLICT - ISRAEL AND PALESTINE

John's use of 'Jews', is a euphemism that he employed for this group only, and not the Jewish nation as a whole. It would be a mistake to create a Christian replacement theology based on a scripture such as this, as many would be apt to do.

There are many more scriptures that will inform the reader of God's continued love and heart for the Jewish people and the nation of Israel.

## Jeremiah 31: 36

*They will never stop being a nation. That would happen only if I lost control of the sun, moon, stars, and the sea." The LORD says, "I will never reject the descendants of Israel. That would happen only if people could measure the sky above, and learn all the secrets of the earth below."*

## Ezekiel 36:24-30

*" 'For I will take you out of the nations; I will gather you from all the countries and bring you back into your own land.*
*I will sprinkle clean water on you, and you will be clean; I will cleanse you from all your impurities and from all your idols.*

*I will give you a new heart and put a new spirit in you; I will remove from you your heart of stone and give you a heart of flesh.*
*And I will put my Spirit in you and move you to follow my decrees and be careful to keep my laws. Then you will live in the land I gave your ancestors; you will be my people, and I will be your God.*
*I will save you from all your uncleanness. I will call for the grain and make it plentiful and will not bring famine upon you.*
*I will increase the fruit of the trees and the crops of the field, so that you will no longer suffer disgrace among the nations because of famine.*

A. He will bring them back to the land and they will be fruitful. Through His power they will make it a garden of Eden.

B. Notice, at first they are still broken, hurting, defensive, prickly and rebellious.

C. He will wash them, heal them and put in them a new spirit and a new heart.

Israel, like the church is still a work in progress. They most definitely are not finished; God is preparing them for part two of Messiah's coming, just as He is for the Church. Part of this preparation is to place them back into the land.

The first part of the promise spoken by the prophet Ezekiel has surely taken place. Even Israel's ememies are in awe of their presence back in the land, and what they have achieved in such a short space of time. Over the past seventy five years, they have indeed been fruitful and much of the land under their control has been completely transformed. The word of God has always proved true, and it will do so in the future as well.

**Romans 11:1**

*I ask then, did God reject His people? Certainly not! I am an Israelite myself, a descendant of Abraham, from the tribe of Benjamin. God did not reject His people, whom He foreknew.*

**Romans 11:11**

*Again I ask: Did they stumble so as to fall beyond recovery? Not at all! Rather, because of their transgression, salvation has come to the Gentiles to make Israel envious. But if their transgression means riches for the world, and their loss means riches for the Gentiles, how much greater riches will their fullness bring!*

## THE CHURCH IS STANDING AT A CROSSROADS

There are two ways to see Israel: from the perspective of the world or from the perspective of God. If we choose the latter, understand though, that this does not involve Christians blindly supporting all that the nation of Israel does or how it acts. As we have seen, they have repeatedly done wrong and like all people have sinned and fallen short of the glory of God.

Yet, neither are we to disregard the power of God's continued covenant promises, by mistakenly thinking that God is finished with Israel, or His need for them to live in the land. We will do so at our own peril. Remember, scriptures inform us that in the last days He will judge all who choose to come against his people, and seek to disassociate them from the land.

## How are we then to respond?

This subject is far greater than just supporting the actions of the nation of Israel, it is about supporting the purposes of the God of Israel. And if that requires us to support the nation of Israel's right to live in the land, so that they are able to fulfil God's eternal purpose of salvation be accomplished, then so be it.

Israel has a divine responsibility to do right. In Romans 13:3, the Apostle Paul speaks to leaders about their responsibility to lead people in a correct way.

*For rulers hold no terror for those who do right, but for those who do wrong. Do you want to be free from fear of the one in authority? Then do what is right and you will be commended.*

On 7th October, Hamas knew what they were doing. They were not just set on committing those atrocities and declaring their intention to eradicate Israel from the land, they were provoking a response. They got one.

Genesis 49:9.

*Judah is a like lion crouching - who dares to rouse him!*

Hamas poked a sleeping lion, and stole her cubs, what did they and the world expect? Israel has gone after Hamas and will not stop until she gets her cubs back, and ensure that Hamas can never attack them again. While many in the world would seek to accuse Israel of genocide for its response, it is only Hamas who has declared the act of genocide to be their intention.

Israel has the right to protect themselves against evil, but in doing so, they must not themselves perpetrate one evil to defeat another evil. Any combat should only be done out of necessity. In fact, this should be applicable to all nations, and not just Israel.

With the need to protect the people of Israel and ensure that such a travesty never ever takes place again, Israel must also root out those who masterminded and perpetrated the evil. Equally, they need to be careful not to punish any innocent people who are under that despotic power.

The problem arises when dealing with wicked enemies who cowardly use innocents as shields, who act inhumanely out of pure hatred, and will continue to do so regardless of the consequences.

Do you stand back and do nothing? This is a perplexing issue!

The ancient Greek philosopher Thucydides said this....

*It is useless to attack men who could not be controlled even if conquered, while failure to do so, would leave us in an even worse position.*

Israel is a part of the continued purposes of God, and it is His heart to establish them and keep them in the land. But equally, the leaders of Israel must have their heart set for him, and seek his authority and righteous ways over all that they do. We pray that they will use their superior power to seek peace and not just retribution.

Jeremiah 32:41.

*I will rejoice in doing them good, and I will plant them in this land in faithfulness, with all my heart and all my soul.*

If we read the chapter 2 Chronicles 20, we can see a powerful Biblical principle in action. Before the King called the people of Israel to lift up weapons, he led them to seek the heart of God.

*After this ithe Moabites and Ammonites, and with them some of the Meunites, came against Jehoshaphat for battle. Some men came and told Jehoshaphat, "A great multitude is coming against you from Edom, from beyond the sea; and, behold, they are in jHazazon-tamar" (that is, kEngedi). Then Jehoshaphat was afraid and set his face lto seek the Lord, and mproclaimed a fast throughout all Judah. And Judah assembled to seek help from the Lord; from all the cities of Judah they came to seek the Lord.*

We believe that it was incumbent on Israel's leadership today, like king Jehoshaphat of old, to publicly call the people of Israel to lift their eyes up to the Lord and call a period of fasting and prayer.

Psalm 20:7

*Some trust in chariots and some in horses, but we trust in the name of the Lord our God.*

# CONCLUSION

Over the course of this study, we have sought to provide a balanced historical and biblical approach to what is a seemingly complex issue. On a human level it would initially appear to be two ancient tribes resurrecting an age-old conflict over a small strip of land and mutual hatred of one another. If we choose to see it this way, it becomes difficult to comprehend how this localised dispute has had such an explosive and volatile effect on the global stage for so many years, and continues to do so.

Examine it in conjunction with the Judeo-Christian biblical narratives, and we are presented with a world view of a super-natural, cosmic battle for the very soul of humanity. At its epicentre, is a strip of land provided to a people group, who become a conduit through which a divine deliverer would be brought forth. The continued presence of people in the land plays an intrinsic part to the ultimate success of the deliverer. God's enemy knowing this does everything to separate them from the land, vilify them and destroy them. If we countenance this viewpoint, and accept that Jesus is the Messiah, it would be important to consider if the New Testament might contain any narratives that would indicate if Jesus held an opinion on Israel's conflict with others.

Interestingly, in Luke 13:1-6, Jesus was asked about his thoughts regarding the massacre of fellow Jews.

*Now on the same occasion there were some present who reported to Him about the Galileans whose blood Pilate had mixed with their sacrifices. And Jesus said to them, "Do you suppose that these Galileans were greater sinners than all other Galileans because they suffered this fate? "I tell you, no, but unless you repent, you will all likewise perish. "Or do you suppose that those eighteen on whom the tower in Siloam fell and killed them were worse culprits than all the men who live in Jerusalem? "I tell you, no, but unless you repent, you will all likewise perish."*

At first glance, this would appear to be a curious response by Jesus, cold and devoid of empathy for the sufferings of his fellow Jews. However, deeper analysis of his comments reveals a consideration that goes beyond physical matters, and demonstrates a profound concern for their spiritual and eternal well-being.  The central focus should not be on the death of the body, but on the spiritual death that will bring eternal separation from God.

God's ultimate purpose for sending His Messiah, is not just to rescue and save Israel from their physical enemies, but to rescue and save the whole world from a greater enemy.

Man's only hope, Jewish or gentile, is to put their trust in the one who God sent to be a blood sacrifice, by shedding his blood on the battlefield of the cross.

Satan, God's cosmic enemy, thought that he had won the battle when Jesus was crucified, but God raised him from the dead so that by His wounds we could be set free and healed once and for all from the mortal virus called sin.

It is sin that is the root cause of wars, anger, violence, bitterness, hatred, jealousy and strife.

We remind ourselves that the first coming of the Messiah was to deal with the power of sin. He also introduced a lifestyle that, if followed, would reduce the negative effects of sin over this world, until He returns to bring ultimate defeat.

We are living in an in-between time, the job is not complete, and Jesus has called us to partner with him to continue to present His kingdom message and kingdom lifestyle to our generation (1Corinthians 3:9).  We need the kingdom to be among us, in us and constantly working through us until Jesus returns to complete the work that He started.

When mankind chooses to reject this message, the result will be the continuation of anger, violence, bitterness, hatred, jealousy, strife and wars. Satan's power will persist and the world will remain under this cloud of darkness. Both Israel and the Church will face constant attack with the aim of destroying the purposes of God.

There are many who would purport that the current problems in Israel and the condition of the world are precursors to the imminent return of the Messiah. We cannot know if current events are leading to the end of times. It may be though, an indication to a day that is coming and we need to remain watchful. The real question is are we ready for that day?

One thing we can be in no doubt of, is that events involving the nation of Israel and the land are significant to the ongoing purposes of God, and His end-time plans. The land belongs to God, and it always will, as it is part of God's eternal purpose to save and restore mankind.

If this is true, then it is incumbent on the Church to support the purposes of the God of Israel for the land and the Jewish people, and not be persuaded by world opinions. This does not mean however, that our eschatological (end times) views involving Israel and its place in biblical prophecy, should make us blind to incorrect decisions or activities of the Israeli political response. Israel is a work in progress and is not flawless.

# FINAL THOUGHTS

a) It is important for Christians to understand that Israel is and always will be central to the eternal purposes of God, and what happens to the people and the land is significant to all of us.

b) You cannot possibly know about Israel, ancient or modern, if you do not know the story of the Bible or its primary theme.

c) The debate regarding Israel and the Palestinians is not merely about two tribes going to war over a piece of land. It is part of a greater battle being played out on a cosmic arena.

While we may have read the back page of the bible, and know that ultimately God is going to win, it does not mean that the battle is not real, or that we sit back and do nothing.

We have been call by God to partner with Him to defeat the works of His enemy in our generation.

We must recognise that this war is being waged is on numerous fronts:

i.   It is for the mind and soul of every human being.
ii.  It is for the identity of God's Church.
iii. It is the integrity and truth of His word.
iv.  It is for true identity of His Messiah, and the power of His work of salvation.
v.   It is for God's continued identity and end-time purposes of Israel.

d) If God's word states that the people of Israel are still a part of His ongoing purposes, and that all believers need to love them, support their biblical right to the land, then this must be acknowledged and adhered to. This does not mean though that Christians blindly support all that Israel as a secular nation does or fail to care for Palestinian people. It is about believers supporting and following the God of Israel, and His purposes. Is it vital that we maintain agreement with God and His word, even if it potentially means that we are in disagreement with the World. Without a correct biblical theology regarding the nation of Israel and the land as seen through God's purposes, our response may not be accurate.

e) The world is broken, full of broken hearts and minds that act and react out of that brokenness. The root of this brokenness is sin. Despite God's intention to eradicate sin, He is not vitriolic, as some might portray Him, but broken-hearted and weeping over the condition of all mankind, regardless of who they are. Our healing of this brokenness starts with contrition and repentance, not rhetoric and violence.

The intention of writing this booklet has been to provide historical information, biblical insights and general observations that will assist all who read it in establishing a balanced, biblical perspective; or, at the very least, to serve as a starting point for further study to help navigate what is for many a moral and spiritual maze.

93

NOTES: